AUTHENTIC READER

A Gateway to Academic English

Faculty of Languages and Cultures
KYUSHU UNIVERSITY

KENKYUSHA

Published in Japan
by Kenkyusha Co., Ltd., Tokyo

Copyright © 2016 by Kyushu University

All rights reserved. No part of this publication may be reproduced or re-used by any means without the prior written permission of the publisher.

はじめに

　本教材は「大学生に本物の英語を読んでもらいたい」との強い思いから開発されました。文理に跨る学際的素材をコンテンツとし、それに実践的な英語スキル及びストラテジーを有機的に統合させて学習することができるように開発された CLIL（内容言語統合型学習）志向の教材です。さらに、教材内のコンテンツに関連する資料をインターネット等から収集し学習することができるようなタスクを加え、自律的な学習能力を涵養することも目指しています。

　本教材を開発するにあたって、まず「大学生が読むべき英文」を収集するという目的で文理を問わず様々な専門分野の大学教員に対してアンケートを行い、その結果を基に英文選定用の書籍を収集しました。さらに、上記調査に加え、英語教育に対するニーズやウォンツ調査、また授業で使われている教科書やタスクについてのアンケートを行い、その結果を開発する教材の「内容」および「言語」の両面に反映させました。

　この教材の活用により、学生は学際的内容を英語で理解し、分析・批判していくという思考活動を主体的に行うことができるようになると期待できます。

本教材使用により期待される効果
(1)「英語を学ぶ授業」から「英語で学ぶ授業」への転換を行い、大学教育の国際化を促進すること。
(2) コンテンツ・ベースの教材を通して、学生自身が文理の領域横断的、多面的・多角的な視点、および分析・批判する方法を学び、学習意欲を高めていくこと。
(3) 専門分野についての情報検索の基礎となる力を養い、高年次英語教育・専門教育にも寄与すること。

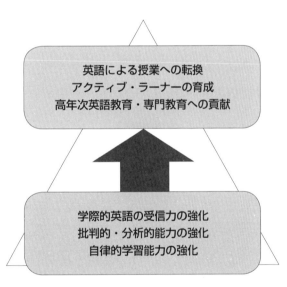

　出版に際しては、研究社の津田正氏、中川京子氏、鈴木美和氏に大変お世話になりました。ここに深く御礼申し上げます。

2016年6月1日
九州大学大学院言語文化研究院 学術英語テキスト編集委員会 著者一同

＊本教材は平成26年度・27年度九州大学教育の質向上支援プログラムによって支援を受けています。

Preface

The development of this textbook has been motivated by our ardent desire to provide university students with an authentic materials textbook. This is a CLIL (Content and Language Integrated Learning)-oriented authentic materials textbook which integrates academic **Contents** covering both humanities and sciences with **Language** tasks intended to develop practical English skills and strategies. It also assigns extension tasks in which students gather data related to the topic contents, encouraging them to learn autonomously.

This textbook has been developed in the following way. First, we sent out a questionnaire to university teachers in various academic fields in order to gather information on English authentic materials being read by university students and on the needs and wants of English teachers. We also made a survey of textbooks used in class and of tasks and assignments given to students. Then, based on the results of these surveys, we selected authentic materials to be used and developed a CLIL-oriented textbook utilizing these materials.

This textbook is expected to improve students' ability to read and comprehend academic English materials and to develop their autonomous attitude to read and analyze critically. It will (1) improve internationalization of the university education by reorienting the teaching approach from "learning English" to "learning in English," (2) enhance students' motivation through studying diverse academic contents and learning methods of critical reading and analyzing, and (3) nourish their fundamental understanding of their specialist fields, contributing to their future careers.

> Conversion to Learning in English
> Developing Active Learners
> Serving as a Gateway to Academic English
>
> ↑
>
> Improving Reading and Listening Ability
> Enhancing Critical and Analytical Ability
> Encouraging Students to Learn Autonomously

We would like to give our sincere thanks to Mr. Tadashi Tsuda, Ms. Kyoko Nakagawa, and Ms. Miwa Suzuki at Kenkyusha. Without their dedicated support, this textbook would not have been published.

June 7, 2016
Academic English Textbook Editorial Committee, Faculty of Languages and Cultures, Kyushu University

*Development of this textbook has been supported by the Kyushu University Enhanced Education Program (EEP) 2014–2015.

執筆者

松村瑞子　大津隆広　内田　諭　下條恵子　岡本太助
横森大輔　土屋智行　志水俊広　Christopher Haswell
Tanya McCarthy　Stephen Laker　Matthew Armstrong
Jonathan Aleles　Michael Guinn

協力者一覧（五十音順）

阿部芳久　一政遼太郎　大河内豊　大橋　浩　岡崎晴輝　小田切顕一　笠井　彩　栗田健一
小室理恵　阪口　慧　志堂寺和則　鈴木右文　隅田康明　田尾周一郎　田崎文得　中村純也
藤井里咲　細見佳子　米本隆裕　山岡　均　渡邉智明　割石博之

本書の構成　　　　　　　　　Book Description

　本書は12のレッスンからなり、人文・社会・自然科学の分野から選ばれた12編のリーディング用テキストが収録されています。「大学生に習得してほしい知識そして思考力とは何か」を念頭において選定されたラインナップとなっています。いずれの英文も教科書用に書かれた文章ではなく、実際の学術活動等のために英語で発表・出版され、世界的にも広く読まれている本格的なものです。また、それぞれのテーマに関連したレクチャー形式のリスニング教材を用意し、それを通して理解や思考をさらに深めることができるよう構成されています。

　This book introduces 12 academic texts from a wide variety of topics, ranging from the humanities to natural science. These 12 mindfully selected texts are written not in "classroom English," but as examples of real-world texts. They are also texts that have earned large audiences with their substantial and authentic contents articulated in academic and readable English. Each lesson is supported by audio lecture content related to the reading passage along with carefully designed exercises, which are both content and language-based. With access to these authentic academic contents and linguistic training, learners can fully expand their academic horizons, improve their critical thinking skills, and develop their fluency in English.

INTRODUCTION

　各レッスンで取り上げる専門分野についての背景知識を紹介しています。英文テキストを読む前に目を通すことで、内容理解の手助けとなるでしょう。

　This introductory section provides the learner with general background information on the academic subject they will learn in the lesson. It will also help them better understand the reading passage.

AIM & OBJECTIVE

　各レッスンの英文テキストが論じる主なテーマと、練習問題を通して習得してほしい言語的スキルを説明しています。

　This section gives the theme and the content of the reading passage and provides a linguistic focus for the lesson.

READING

◆ Key Words & Phrases

　各レッスンの英文テキストに登場する専門用語を解説しています。リーディングとリスニングの内容をよく理解する上で必要な語句を選びました。

　Each lesson introduces the key terminology of the text, those that are essential to understand the reading and listening materials. This section offers a glossary for this content-related vocabulary.

◆ Pre-class Task

英文テキストを読んだ後に基本的な内容把握の確認を行うための正誤問題です。授業前に予習課題として解いてもよいですし、授業内で出題される場合もあるでしょう。

True / False questions in this section are designed to test the learner's general understanding of the reading passage. Students can check their understanding of the passage before class, and the instructors can use them in class to organize the comprehension activities related to the text.

◆ In-class Task

Warm-up

授業に積極的に参加するためのウォームアップとして、レッスンで取り上げるテーマに関連したトピックを提示しています。ペアまたは少人数のグループで話し合ってみましょう。

This is a mini discussion related to the topic of the lesson, designed to open up the learner's mind and direct their attention towards the additional activities of the class.

Reading Comprehension

英文テキストに関するパラグラフごとの内容把握問題です。各パラグラフの要旨、あるいは重要なポイントについて確認する問題となっています。基本的には記述式のタスクとなっており、解答を英語で組み立てるための論理的思考力や表現力を磨くための練習問題でもあります。

In this section, questions arranged paragraph-by-paragraph are designed to check the learner's understanding of the reading passage. They cover the main ideas and important details of each paragraph in sequence. These questions are basically description-type and thus require the learner to construct logically and linguistically correct answers.

LISTENING

Before You Listen

授業内でのリスニング・アクティヴィティーに積極的に参加するためのウォームアップとして、レッスンで取り上げる内容に関連したトピックを提示しています。ペアまたは少人数のグループで話し合ってみましょう。

This is a mini discussion related to the topic of the listening material, designed to direct the learners' attentions to the further listening activities in class.

Word Focus

実際のリスニングに入る前に、トピックに関する重要語とその定義や例文をリストアップするアクティヴィティーです。トピックに関連する重要語句を事前に学んでおくことで、リスニング時の内容理解が深まります。授業前の予習課題にするとよいでしょう。

This section requires the learner to predict some important words related to the topic of the listening section and list them. The learner should also write the definitions of those words or build sentences using them. Learning words before listening can help the learner fully understand the content of the listening. This section will work well as a pre-class assignment.

Listening 1: Short Summary

レッスンのトピックに関するレクチャーを聴き、短い英文概要の空欄を埋めるアクティヴィティーです。これによって、学習者はリスニング内容の概略を把握することができ、より詳細な理解・考察のための足がかりを得ることができます。

The learner listens to a lecture related to the lesson topic and completes the summary of the listening passage using the words provided. This activity helps the learner understand the general outline of the passage and prepare to explore it at a deeper level with the following activities.

Listening 2: Question & Answer

再び同じレクチャーを聴き、各パラグラフの要旨、あるいは重要なポイントについて確認していきます。基本的に記述式のタスクとなっており、解答を英語で組み立てるための論理的思考力や表現力も鍛えられます。テキスト内にはノート・テイキング用のスペースも設けられており、ノート・テイキングの練習も行うことができます。

The learner listens to the passage again and answers more detailed questions here. They are basically description-type questions and thus require the learner to construct answers that are logically and linguistically correct. This section also provides a blank space for note taking so that the learner can practice how to take notes while listening to the lecture.

True / False

レクチャーの内容把握の確認として正誤問題を解きます。先ほどのノート・テイキングを基にして解答し、レクチャーの内容の重要なポイントを再度確認します。ペアまたは少人数のグループで話し合ってみましょう。

This is a wrap-up activity for the listening section. The learner answers True / False questions based on the notes they previously took. Student's decisions regarding their answers can also be discussed with a partner or in a small group. Through such questions the learner can review the main points and significant details of the listening passage.

DISCUSSION

各レッスンの総括となるクラス規模のディスカッションであり、学習者はそのレッスンで学んだことを基に自分の意見を述べます。提示されているトピックは各レッスンのリーディング・リスニングに関するもので、学習者の批判的思考能力の向上を意図して作成されています。

This is a whole-class discussion based on what the learner has learned in the lesson. A discussion topic is related to the central issue of the lesson and designed to develop the learner's critical thinking.

A STEP FORWARD

各レッスンに関連する発展的トピックについて調べ、記述する練習問題です。内容に関連する資料をインターネット等から収集し、必要な情報を組み合わせて解答を作成します。授業後の自習課題として、学習者のより発展的な自律学習を促します。

This task is designed as a post-class assignment. The learner is directed to investigate technical terms or special topics related to the contents of the lesson using the Internet or other media, and to gather essential pieces of information to construct answers in their own words. The task aims to stimulate interest in academic research and encourage post-class autonomous learning.

FURTHER READING

学習者が学術的な興味および思考をさらに発展させることができるような文献リストを掲載しています。文献ごとに短い解説をつけ、授業外での知的意欲に応える読書案内となっています。

This offers reading lists to the learner in order for them to cultivate their academic interests and develop their scholarly mindsets after class or after the entire course. Short annotations along with book information are also provided to assist students in finding texts that best match their area of interest in the topic.

音声について

本書の音声データ（MP3）は、研究社ウェブサイト（http://www.kenkyusha.co.jp）から、以下の手順でダウンロードできます。

(1) 研究社ウェブサイトのトップページで「音声ダウンロード」をクリックして「音声データダウンロード書籍一覧」のページに移動してください。

(2) 移動したページの「Authentic Reader: A Gateway to Academic English」の紹介欄に「ダウンロード」ボタンがあります。クリックすると、ユーザー名とパスワードの入力が求められますので、以下のように入力してください。
ユーザー名：guest
パスワード：AuthenticReaderDownload

(3) ユーザー名とパスワードが正しく入力されると、ファイルのダウンロードが始まります。ダウンロード完了後、解凍してご利用ください。

The sound files (in MP3 format) for this textbook can be downloaded from the publisher's website.

(1) Go to http://www.kenkyusha.co.jp and then click "音声ダウンロード" from the page menu. This will take you a list of books whose listening data files are available online.

(2) Find the textbook "Authentic Reader: A Gateway to Academic English" from the list and click the "ダウンロード" (Download) button. The following information will be necessary to download the data:
User Name: guest
Password: AuthenticReaderDownload

(3) You will need to unzip the folder containing the downloaded files before you can use the MP3 files.

［音声ナレーション］
Chris Koprowski
Jessica Kozuka
Michael Rhys

目次　　　　　　　　　　　　　　　　　Table of Contents

はじめに ……………………………………………………………… iii

本書の構成 …………………………………………………………… vi

LESSON 1　Paper Books or E-books ……………………………… 1

LESSON 2　Pursuit of Happiness in Economics ………………… 13

LESSON 3　What Is Natural Selection? …………………………… 25

LESSON 4　Power in World Politics ……………………………… 36

LESSON 5　Intelligent Transportation Systems ………………… 47

LESSON 6　Language and Thought ……………………………… 60

LESSON 7　Silent Spring …………………………………………… 71

LESSON 8　The U.S. Civil Rights Movement …………………… 82

LESSON 9　Human Genes ………………………………………… 92

LESSON 10　Women's Rights Are Human Rights ……………… 104

LESSON 11　Black Holes and Astronomical Wonders ………… 115

LESSON 12　What Is Literature? ………………………………… 126

LESSON 1　Paper Books or E-books

INTRODUCTION

　若者が読書しなくなったと言われ始めて久しいですが、これは多くの場合、本や雑誌や新聞といった印刷物を読まなくなったことを指しています。ところが、「読書」の範囲を拡げて、PCのブラウザやスマートフォン上などで読む文字情報も含めるとすれば、読書量はむしろ増えているという試算もあります。特に電子書籍の普及は、読書のあり方を大きく変える可能性を秘めていますし、すでにそうした変化が起きていることも明らかです。日本でも、2010年が「電子書籍元年」と呼ばれており、紙からスクリーンへ、インクから電子的ドットへと、読書のあり方は急激に変化してきています。

　紙に印刷されたものを読む方がよいのか、あるいは電子媒体で読む方がよいのか、近年出版界を二分する議論がなされています。これらの読書形態に「違い」があることは広く認識されていますが、具体的にどう違うのかを理解している人は少ないようです。紙媒体を用いる読書が電子媒体での読書に取って代わられる日が来るかどうかは分かりませんが、両者の違いを理解することで、より充実した読書体験が得られるかもしれません。

AIM & OBJECTIVE

CONTENT

　このレッスンでは、紙媒体のテキストを読む場合と電子媒体のテキストを読む場合の違いについて考えます。文字情報を「読む」という点では同じですが、テキストと読者の身体の関係性や、文字と情報の認知の仕方については、かなり違いがあることが近年の研究から明らかになっています。

LANGUAGE

　英文テキストの中から必要な情報を素早く探し出す練習を行います。「スキャニング（scanning）」というテクニックを用いて、特定の単語や数字などを見つけ出し、その周辺を詳しく読んでみましょう。また、リスニングではこのレッスンのトピックに関する講義を聞き、内容理解や要約などの訓練を行います。

READING: Why the Brain Prefers Paper

◆ Key Words & Phrases

medium	媒体。複数形は media. パソコンやタブレットなどを指すが、物理的な「機器 (device)」というよりは、それらの機能に着目する呼び方。
letter / character	文字。letter の場合は、ある文字を特定の音や意味を表す記号として捉え、character の場合は、文字の形状に注目する。
representation	表象（ひょうしょう）。特定の対象を他のもの（言葉や画像など）で表現したもの。例えば、友人の顔を思い浮かべる場合は、その脳内のイメージが実在の友人の表象となる。
topography	空間的構造、位置関係。屋外の地形の高低差やランドマークの位置、屋内の家具の配置など、空間を認識する際に参照する様々な特徴のこと。

[1] One of the most provocative viral YouTube videos in the past two years begins mundanely enough: a one-year-old girl plays with an iPad, sweeping her fingers across its touch screen and shuffling groups of icons. In following scenes, she appears to pinch, swipe, and prod the pages of paper magazines as though they, too, are screens. Melodramatically, the video replays these gestures in close-up.

[2] For the girl's father, the video—*A Magazine Is an iPad That Does Not Work*—is evidence of a generational transition. In an accompanying description, he writes, "Magazines are now useless and impossible to understand, for digital natives"—that is, for people who have been interacting with digital technologies from a very early age, surrounded not only by paper books and magazines but also by smartphones, Kindles, and iPads.

[3] Whether or not his daughter truly expected the magazines to behave like an iPad, the video brings into focus a question that is relevant to far more than the

---

出典：Jabr, Ferris. 2013. "Why the Brain Prefers Paper." *Scientific American*, Volume 309, No 5. pp. 48–53.（邦訳：「デジタルより紙がわかりやすい理由」『日経サイエンス』2014年4月号、日経サイエンス社）作者のジャブル氏はアメリカのオレゴン州在住のライターで、元 *Scientific American* 誌の編集者だった人物。この記事は、2014年度版 *The Best American Science and Nature Writing* (Boston: Houghton Mifflin Harcourt) にも収録されている。

[1] **viral** 「ウィルス (virus) 性の」情報が口コミなどを通して、ネットワーク上で広範囲に急速に拡散する様子を伝染病に喩えた表現。
[2] **mundanely enough** 「ごく平凡に、ごくありふれた感じで」
[5] **melodramatically** ドラマチックな編集・演出がなされているということ。
[12] **whether or not ...** 「…かどうかはともかく」
[13] **bring ... into focus** 「…に焦点を当てる」それまであまり注目されなかったものを前面に出して目立たせること。
[13] **relevant to ...** 「…に関係のある、…にとって重要な」

youngest among us: How exactly does the technology we use to read change the way we read?

4. Since at least the 1980s researchers in psychology, computer engineering, and library and information science have published more than one hundred studies exploring differences in how people read on paper and on screens. Before 1992 most experiments concluded that people read stories and articles on screens more slowly and remember less about them. As the resolution of screens on all kinds of devices sharpened, however, a more mixed set of findings began to emerge. Recent surveys suggest that although most people still prefer paper—especially when they need to concentrate for a long time—attitudes are changing as tablets and e-reading technology improve and as reading digital texts for facts and fun becomes more common. In the United States, e-books currently make up more than 20 percent of all books sold to the general public.

5. Despite all the increasingly user-friendly and popular technology, most studies published since the early 1990s confirm earlier conclusions: paper still has advantages over screens as a reading medium. Together, laboratory experiments, polls, and consumer reports indicate that digital devices prevent people from efficiently navigating long texts, which may subtly inhibit reading comprehension. Compared with paper, screens may also drain more of our mental resources while we are reading and make it a little harder to remember what we read when we are done. Whether they realize it or not, people often approach computers and tablets with a state of mind less conducive to learning than the one they bring to paper. And e-readers fail to re-create certain tactile experiences of reading on paper, the absence of which some find unsettling.

6. Understanding how reading on paper differs from reading on screens requires some explanation of how the human brain interprets written language. Although letters and words are symbols representing sounds and ideas, the brain also regards them as physical objects. As Maryanne Wolf of Tufts University explains in her 2007 book *Proust and the Squid*, we are not born with brain circuits

---

[7] **resolution** 「(電子機器の画面の) 解像度」
[8] **mixed** 「(賛否、肯定と否定などが) 入り混じった」
[11] **for facts and fun** 「情報収集や楽しみのために」
[12] **make up** 「(ある割合) を占める」
[18] **navigate** 「読み進める」本来は船舶や航空機が航路を進むこと。
[22] **conducive to ...** 「…を助ける、…に役立つ」
[23] **tactile** 「触覚の」本を手に持ったときの手触りや重みを指している。
[24] **unsettling** 「落ち着かない気持ちにさせる」
[28] **physical** 「物理的な」mental (心理的な) の対義語として用いられている。
[29] **circuit** 「(脳の) 神経回路」

dedicated to reading, because we did not invent writing until relatively recently in our evolutionary history, around the fourth millennium B.C. So in childhood the brain improvises a brand-new circuit for reading by weaving together various ribbons of neural tissue devoted to other abilities, such as speaking, motor coordination, and vision.

7. Some of these repurposed brain regions specialize in object recognition: they help us instantly distinguish an apple from an orange, for example, based on their distinct features, yet classify both as fruit. Similarly, when we learn to read and write, we begin to recognize letters by their particular arrangements of lines, curves, and hollow spaces—a tactile learning process that requires both our eyes and our hands. In recent research by Karin James of Indiana University Bloomington, the reading circuits of five-year-old children crackled with activity when they practiced writing letters by hand but not when they typed letters on a keyboard. And when people read cursive writing or intricate characters such as Japanese *kanji*, the brain literally goes through the motions of writing, even if the hands are empty.

8. Beyond treating individual letters as physical objects, the human brain may also perceive a text in its entirety as a kind of physical landscape. When we read, we construct a mental representation of the text. The exact nature of such representations remains unclear, but some researchers think they are similar to the mental maps we create of terrain—such as mountains and trails—and of indoor physical spaces, such as apartments and offices. Both anecdotally and in published studies, people report that when trying to locate a particular passage in a book, they often remember where in the text it appeared. Much as we might recall that we passed the red farmhouse near the start of a hiking trail before we started climbing uphill through the forest, we remember that we read about Mr. Darcy rebuffing Elizabeth Bennet at a dance on the bottom left corner of the left-hand page in one of the earlier chapters of Jane Austen's *Pride and Prejudice*.

[3]　**improvise**　「即席で作り出す」
[4]　**neural tissue**　「脳神経組織」
[5]　**motor coordination**　「(身体部位の間での) 運動の連携」生理学では、motor は身体の運動を指す。
[6]　**repurposed**　「別の新たな目的のために用いられる、新たな役割を与えられた」
[12]　**crackle with activity**　「活発に活動する」
[21]　**mental map**　「メンタルマップ」人の記憶の中に描かれる主観的な地図。
[22]　**anecdotally**　anecdote は「逸話、エピソード」で、裏づけとなる証拠がない発言のこと。実験によって再現したり確かめたりすることができないため、科学的ではないとみなされる。
[24]　**much as we might recall that …**　「…を思い出すのと同じように」後半の we remember that … につながる。
[28]　**Jane Austen**　イギリスの小説家 (1775–1817)。*Pride and Prejudice* (1813) はオースティンの代表作で、ジェインとエリザベスの姉妹の恋愛と結婚をめぐる小説。

9 In most cases, paper books have more obvious topography than on-screen text. An open paper book presents a reader with two clearly defined domains—the left- and right-hand pages—and a total of eight corners with which to orient oneself. You can focus on a single page of a paper book without losing awareness of the whole text. You can even feel the thickness of the pages you have read in one hand and the pages you have yet to read in the other. Turning the pages of a paper book is like leaving one footprint after another on a trail—there is a rhythm to it and a visible record of how far one has traveled. All these features not only make the text in a paper book easily navigable, they also make it easier to form a coherent mental map of that text.

10 In contrast, most digital devices interfere with intuitive navigation of a text and inhibit people from mapping the journey in their mind. A reader of digital text might scroll through a seamless stream of words, tap forward one page at a time, or use the search function to immediately locate a particular phrase—but it is difficult to see any one passage in the context of the entire text. As an analogy, imagine if Google Maps allowed people to navigate street by individual street, as well as teleport to any specific address, but prevented them from zooming out to see a neighborhood, state, or country. Likewise, glancing at a progress bar gives a far more vague sense of place than feeling the weight of read and unread pages. And although e-readers and tablets replicate pagination, the displayed pages are ephemeral. Once read, those pages vanish. Instead of hiking the trail yourself, you watch the trees, rocks, and moss pass by in flashes, with no tangible trace of what came before and no easy way to see what lies ahead. *(1172 words)*

---

[2] **domain** 「(他とはっきり区別された) 領域」
[3] **orient oneself** 「(読者が) 自分の現在位置を確認する」
[6] **you have yet to read** 「これから読む、まだ読んでいない」
[16] **street by individual street** 「通り (街区) ごとに」
[18] **progress bar** 「プログレスバー」電子書籍リーダーで本のどのあたりを読んでいるかを示す。
[20] **pagination** 「ページ番号を振ること、ページに分けた表示」紙の書籍の形態を電子機器上で再現するということ。
[23] **tangible** 「触れる (触れて確かめる) ことができる、はっきりした形のある」

• LESSON 1 •

◆ Pre-class Task
Read the passage above. Mark each sentence as T (True) or F (False).

☞ 1 - 3

1. The episode of the young girl on the YouTube video is used by the writer to show that there is a problem unique to younger generations. (   )

☞ 4

2. Technological development after the 1990s changed the way researchers think about the differences between paper books and e-books. (   )

☞ 5

3. Recent studies show that we remember what we read more clearly when reading it on paper than on screens. (   )

☞ 6

4. At birth, we have a part of our brain that specializes in reading. (   )

☞ 7

5. For both reading and writing we use the same parts of our brains. (   )

☞ 8

6. Researchers understand everything about how the brain creates a mental map when we read. (   )

☞ 9 - 10

7. E-books give us clearer idea of our progression through the text. (   )

☞ 10

8. E-books are similar to Google Maps because neither allows us to see the whole text or map. (   )

● Paper Books or E-books ●

◆ In-class Task

💬 Warm-up

List advantages and disadvantages of paper books and e-books. Then compare your results with your partner's.

	Advantages	Disadvantages
Paper books		
E-books		

✏️ Reading Comprehension

☞ 2

1. What is a "digital native?" Read the text and write a definition.
   _____
   _____

☞ 4 - 5

2. A) What are the "earlier conclusions?" B) Why did researchers confirm the "earlier conclusions" after the 1990s? Find at least three reasons in the text.

   A) The "earlier conclusions" are _____
   _____
   _____

   B) Reasons: _____
   _____
   _____
   _____
   _____

7

• LESSON 1 •

☞ 6 - 7

3. What does it mean that the brain recognizes letters as "physical objects?" Scan the text to find the part that explains this and write it down.

_____
_____
_____

☞ 8 - 10

4. The author argues that *reading is like traveling*. Scan the text and list up the similarities between these two activities.

_____
_____
_____
_____
_____

☞ 10

5. A) What does the statement "the displayed pages are ephemeral" mean?
   B) What can be inferred from this about the author's opinion on e-reading?
   A) It means that _____
   _____
   B) The author believes that _____
   _____
   _____

LISTENING: The End of Paper Books?

 Before You Listen

Match the words in the Word Bank to the upper or lower part of the brain.

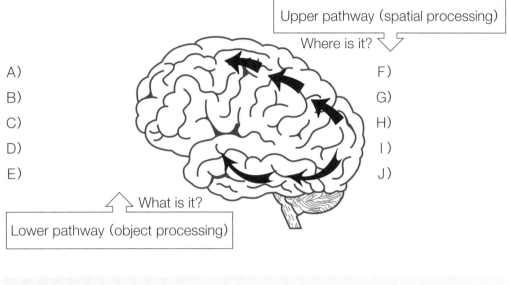

A)
B)
C)
D)
E)

F)
G)
H)
I)
J)

Word Bank

location   sizes   movement   directions   colors   picture details   spacing
range   textures   shapes

Word Focus

Here are 5 key words used in the listening. Look online and find a real-life example of how these words are used in context. Write the **sentences** below.

neuroscience (n.)	
encyclopedia (n.)	
process (v.)	
interactive (adj.)	
nostalgia (n.)	

• LESSON 1 •

🎧 Listening 1: Short Summary

Listen to the passage and complete this summary of the listening using the following words in their correct forms (use 4 of the 5 words).

> digital (adj.)   generation (n.)   neural (adj.)   ink and paper (adj.)
> changing (adj.)

Today's _____ of readers have been brought up in a _____ world in which _____ books have taken the place of the more traditional _____ method of assimilating knowledge.

🎧 Listening 2: Question & Answer

Listen again to the passage and answer the following questions. You can use the box below to write notes. They will help you to answer the questions.

1. What are some examples of reading materials and activities of the speaker's generation?
   _____
   _____

2. According to the speaker, what does the "visual cortex" part of the brain do?
   _____

3. The speaker talks about two different pathways in our brains that help us to understand text: the ventral pathway and the dorsal pathway. Where in the brain are they located?
   _____
   _____

4. What argument does the speaker introduce to explain why some people use e-books when paper books help us to understand more quickly?
   _____

5. In what ways does the speaker feel nostalgic about printed books?
   _____
   _____

Notes	Tip: When comparing different categories, it is a good idea to divide into sections.
Pathway 1: _____ Main ideas:	Ink and paper Main ideas:
Pathway 2: _____ Main ideas:	E-books Main ideas:

True / False

Using your notes, discuss with your partner whether the following statements are true or false. Circle the correct answer and explain your decision.

1. The speaker argues that the age of reading printed books is over.   True False

2. The speaker explains that the brain processes printed books and e-books in the same way.   True False

3. The speaker feels that there is some merit in learning from e-books.   True False

4. The speaker feels excited about the rapid changes in the world of reading.   True False

5. The speaker says that both young and old generations feel nostalgic about books.   True False

DISCUSSION

Do you prefer paper books or e-books? Discuss with your partner and give at least three reasons for your preference. Use the list you created in the "Warm-up" activity at the beginning of the reading section.

_____
_____
_____

● LESSON 1 ●

A STEP FORWARD

Look up the following word online, define what it is and explain how it works.
　E-ink

_____

_____

FURTHER READING

［1］大原ケイ（2010）。『ルポ　電子書籍大国アメリカ』アスキー・メディアワークス。
［2］マーコスキー、ジェイソン（2014）。『本は死なない―Amazonキンドル開発者が語る「読書の未来」』浅川佳秀訳、講談社。
［3］歌田明弘（2010）。『電子書籍の時代は本当に来るのか』筑摩書房。

［1］は、ニューヨーク在住の日本人出版エージェントによる、アメリカ合衆国での電子書籍をめぐる状況についての報告。書籍の出版・流通のメカニズムが、それに直接関わる立場から解説されており、アメリカにおける読書のあり方やその出版文化の独特さが、日本の場合と比較して述べられていて、比較文化論としても興味深く読むことができる。［2］は、初代キンドル（アマゾン社の電子書籍端末）の開発者による、読書のデジタル化によってもたらされる未来の読書体験についての論考。書物や読書の歴史についても丁寧に説明がなされており、書物のデジタル化は書物を破壊するものではなく、読書をいまいちど有意義なものにするという見方が示されている。［3］は、タイトル通りに電子書籍の普及についてやや懐疑的な立場から論じたものである。アップル、アマゾン、グーグルなどの主な取り組みが紹介され、それらがはらむ問題点を日本のケースと対比させながら、電子書籍によって引き起こされる社会と文化の変化についての考察がなされている。

LESSON 2 Pursuit of Happiness in Economics

INTRODUCTION

　経済学の中でもミクロ経済学は、個人の意思決定が「自分が得をするように、あるいは損をしないように」という「合理性」のもとに行われている、と考える学問です。この観点は、人間を私利私欲でしか物事を判断できない存在だと捉えているようにも見えますが、実際はもっと複雑なものです。この「得をする」という感覚は、言い換えれば「満足を味わう」という感覚であり、例えば、他人が

幸せになることで自分も幸せになる個人を想定すれば、ボランティア活動や寄付行動も、その人が「得をするため」に行った「合理的行動」となるのです。

　ミクロ経済学では、個人が対価を支払って、財（商品や有料のサービス）を消費するときに得られる満足度を「効用（utility）」と呼び、どのような消費活動が個々人の効用を最大化するかが研究されます。何を幸福と感じるのか、人によって千差万別であるのと同様に、どのような消費活動が人に満足感をもたらすのかも千差万別です。その違いの背後にはどのような要因があるのでしょうか。

AIM & OBJECTIVE

CONTENT

　このレッスンでは、経済学における「効用の最大化」について考えます。「効用の最大化」とは私たちが消費を通して得ることのできる満足度をできるだけ大きくする、ということですが、それは必ずしも個人が物質的欲求を満たすことを指すとは限りません。「効用の最大化」にはどのようなものがあるのか見ていきましょう。

LANGUAGE

　文章中に登場する「言い換え（paraphrasing）」に注目します。「言い換え」は読者が抽象的な概念を具体的に理解することを助けたり、一般的な事象について学術用語を用いて説明し読者に用語の理解や定着を促したりします。また、リスニングではこのレッスンのトピックに関する講義を聞き、内容理解や要約などの訓練を行います。

● LESSON 2 ●

READING: Utility and Preferences

◆ Key Words & Phrases

Chicago Coalition for the Homeless	ホームレスの人々や専門家が協力し、ホームレス問題を予防・根絶するために、1980年に設立されたシカゴのネットワーク組織。アメリカ全国組織 (National Coalition for the Homeless) の下部組織でもある。
World Bank	世界銀行。各国の中央政府または同政府から債務保証を受けた機関に対し融資を行う等、第二次世界大戦後の金融制度秩序の中心を担う国際機関。1944年創設。
utility	「効用」を意味する経済用語。集合名詞。人が財（人間の欲望を満たす商品や有料サービス）を消費することから得られる満足の度合い、あるいは使用価値を表す。哲学などの分野では「幸福」、「功利」と訳されることもある。また、経済学や哲学以外の一般的な場面では、可算名詞として（主に複数形 utilities という形で）ガス・水道・電気・電話などの「諸設備」を指す。例えば、utility bills とはガス代、水道代などの「公共料金」を意味する語であり、日常的に使用される表現である。

[1] Gary Becker, a University of Chicago economist who won the Nobel Prize in 1992, has noted (borrowing from George Bernard Shaw) that "economy is the art of making the most of life." Economics is the study of how we do that. There is a finite supply of everything worth having: oil, coconut milk, perfect bodies, clean water, people who can fix jammed photocopy machines, etc. How do we allocate these things? Why is it that Bill Gates owns a private jet and you don't? He is rich, you might answer. But why is he rich? Why does he have a larger claim on the world's finite resources than everyone else? At the same time, how

[5]

出典：Wheelan, Charles. 2010. *Naked Economics: Undressing the Dismal Science*. (Fully revised and updated). New York: Norton. pp. 6–8. （邦訳：山形浩生・守岡桜訳『経済学をまる裸にする―本当はこんなに面白い』日本経済新聞社）著者 C. ウィーランはシカゴ大学やダートマス大学などで教鞭をとる傍ら、新聞 *Chicago Tribune* や *The New York Times* などにも多くの経済関連記事を寄稿してきたアメリカの経済学者である。本著は難解な経済学の応用研究を面白くかつ分かりやすく紹介した一般向けの書籍であり、現在13ヶ国語に翻訳され、世界で広く読まれる人気の入門書となっている。

[2] **George Barnard Shaw** アイルランド生まれのイギリスの劇作家・批評家（1856–1950）。*Man and Superman* (1903) や、映画『マイ・フェア・レディ』の原作 *Pygmalion* (1912) などが有名。
[2] **the art of making the most of life** 「人生をできるだけ有意義に過ごすための技」
[4] **finite** 「有限の、制限のある」
[5] **jammed** 「コピー用紙の詰まった」
[6] **allocate** 「分配する、割り当てる」
[6] **Why is it that . . . ?** 「…なのはどういう訳なのだろうか」
[6] **Bill Gates** アメリカ Microsoft 社の創立者（1955– ）。
[8] **claim** 「権利、資格」
[8] **how is it possible that . . .** 「いったいどうして…のようなことが可能なのだろうか」

is it possible in a country as rich as the United States—a place where Alex Rodriguez can be paid $275 million to play baseball—that one in five children is poor or that some adults are forced to rummage through garbage cans for food? Near my home in Chicago, the Three Dog Bakery sells cakes and pastries *only for dogs*. Wealthy professionals pay $16 for birthday cakes for their pets. Meanwhile, the Chicago Coalition for the Homeless estimates that fifteen thousand people are homeless on any given night in that same city.

2 These kinds of disparities grow even more pronounced as we look beyond the borders of the United States. Three-quarters of the people in Chad have no access to clean drinking water, let alone pastries for their pets. The World Bank estimates that half of the world's population survives on less than $2 a day. How does it all work—or, in some cases, not work?

3 Economics starts with one very important assumption: <u>Individuals act to make themselves as well off as possible</u>. To use the jargon of the profession, individuals seek to maximize their own utility, which is a similar concept to happiness, only broader. I derive utility from getting a typhoid immunization and paying taxes. Neither of these things makes me particularly happy, but they do keep me from dying of typhoid or going to jail. That, in the long run, makes me better off. Economists don't particularly care what gives us utility; they simply accept that each of us has his or her own "preferences." I like coffee, old houses, classic films, dogs, bicycling, and many other things. Everyone else in the world has preferences, which may or may not have anything in common with mine.

4 Indeed, this seemingly simple observation that different individuals have different preferences is sometimes lost on otherwise sophisticated policymakers. For example, rich people have different preferences than poor people do.

---

[1] **Alex Rodriguez**　アメリカの有名プロ野球選手（1975– ）。
[3] **rummage**　「くまなく捜す、かきまわして捜す」
[5] **professional**　「専門家」弁護士や医師等の知的専門職に就く人を指すことが多い。
[7] **on any given night**　「どの夜でも、毎晩」
[8] **disparity**　「格差、不平等」
[8] **pronounced**　「明白な、著しい」
[9] **Chad**　「チャド共和国」アフリカ中北部の内陸国。
[10] **let alone ...**　「…は言うまでもなく」
[11] **How does it all work?**　「これはいったいどういう仕組みになっているのだろう」
[13] **assumption**　「仮定、仮説」
[14] **well off**　「裕福な、状況的にうまくいっている」
[14] **jargon**　「専門用語」
[16] **typhoid immunization**　「チフスの予防注射」
[18] **better off**　「より裕福な、より幸せな」
[24] **otherwise**　「その他の点では」
[24] **policymaker**　「政策立案者」

Similarly, our individual preferences may change over the course of our life cycle as we (we hope) grow wealthier. The phrase "luxury good" actually has a technical meaning to economists; it is a good that we buy in increasing quantities as we grow richer—things like sports cars and French wines. Less obviously, concern for the environment is a luxury good. Wealthy Americans are willing to spend more money to protect the environment *as a fraction of their incomes* than are less wealthy Americans. The same relationship holds true across countries; wealthy nations devote a greater share of their resources to protecting the environment than do poor countries. The reason is simple enough: We care about the fate of the Bengal tiger *because we can*. We have homes and jobs and clean water and birthday cakes for our dogs.

5 Here is a nettlesome policy question: Is it fair for those of us who live comfortably to impose our preferences on individuals in the developing world? Economists argue that it is not, though we do it all the time. When I read a story in the Sunday *New York Times* about South American villagers cutting down virgin rain forest and destroying rare ecosystems, I nearly knock over my Starbucks latte in surprise and disgust. But I am not they. My children are not starving or at risk of dying from malaria. If they were, and if chopping down a valuable wildlife habitat enabled me to afford to feed my family and buy a mosquito net, then I would sharpen my ax and start chopping. I wouldn't care how many butterflies or spotted weasels I killed. This is not to suggest that the environment in the developing world does not matter. It does. In fact, there are many examples of environmental degradation that will make poor countries even poorer in the long run. Cutting down those forests is bad for the rest of us, too, since deforestation is a major contributor to rising CO_2 emissions. (Economists often argue that rich countries ought to pay poor countries to protect natural resources that have global value.)

6 Obviously if the developed world were more generous, then Brazilian villagers

---

[2] **luxury good** 「贅沢品」
[3] **a good that we buy in increasing quantities as we grow richer** 「裕福になるにつれてより多く購入するようになる商品」
[12] **nettlesome** 「いらいらさせられる」
[13] **impose** 「押しつける、負わせる、課す」
[19] **habitat** 「生息地」
[20] **ax** 「斧」axeと綴ることも多い。
[21] **weasel** 「イタチ」
[23] **degradation** 「退化、低落、悪化」
[25] **emission** 「排出量、排気」
[28] **generous** 「物惜しみしない、気前のよい」

might not have to decide between destroying the rain forest and buying mosquito nets. For now, the point is more basic: It is simply bad economics to impose our preferences on individuals whose lives are much, much different.

7 Let me make one <u>other important point regarding our individual preferences</u>: Maximizing utility is not synonymous with acting selfishly. In 1999, the *New York Times* published the obituary of Oseola McCarty, a woman who died at the age of ninety-one after spending her life working as a laundress in Hattiesburg, Mississippi. She had lived alone in a small, sparsely furnished house with a black-and-white television that received only one channel. What made Ms. McCarty exceptional is that she was by no means poor. In fact, four years before her death she gave away $150,000 to the University of Southern Mississippi—a school that she had never attended—to endow a scholarship for poor students.

8 Does Oseola McCarty's behavior turn the field of economics on its head? Are Nobel Prizes being recalled to Stockholm? No. She simply derived more utility from saving her money and eventually giving it away than she would have from spending it on a big-screen TV or a fancy apartment. *(999 words)*

---

[2] **for now** 「今のところ、さしあたって」
[5] **synonymous** 「同じ意味合いの、類義語の」
[6] **obituary** 「死亡記事、訃報」
[7] **laundress** 「洗濯屋」洗濯・アイロンがけを職とする女性を指す。
[10] **exceptional** 「異例な、別格の、ひときわすぐれた」
[10] **by no means** 「決して…ではない」
[12] **school** 「大学」アメリカ英語では大学も school と呼ぶことが多い。
[12] **endow** 「与える、（学校や病院などに）財産を寄付する」
[13] **turn the field of economics on its head** 「経済学の世界を覆す、混乱させる」
[14] **recall** 「回収する」
[16] **fancy** 「高級な」

● LESSON 2 ●

◆ Pre-class Task

Read the passage above. Mark each sentence as T (True) or F (False).

☞ 1

1. The author compares the homeless problem in Chicago with the availability of expensive pet food. (   )

☞ 2

2. More than half of the population in Chad has no access to clean drinking water. (   )

☞ 3

3. What gives us utility varies among individuals, and those differences are called "preferences." (   )

☞ 4

4. Sports cars and French wines are luxury goods, but environmental awareness is not. (   )

☞ 5

5. The author seems sympathetic toward those who need to cut down trees to support their families. (   )

☞ 6

6. The author states that it is not a good idea to impose one's preferences on others living in a different situation. (   )

☞ 7-8

7. Ms. McCarty lived a simple life and saved to endow a scholarship for poor students studying at her old school. (   )

• Pursuit of Happiness in Economics •

◆ In-class Task

🗨 Warm-up

Work in pairs. Tell each other from which things you derive greatest utility in your life?

✏ Reading Comprehension

☞ 1

1. Which of the following are mentioned by the author as examples of wealthy professionals/establishments?
   A) Gary Becker
   B) George Bernard Shaw
   C) Bill Gates
   D) Alex Rodriguez
   E) Three Dog Bakery
   F) Chicago Coalition for the Homeless

☞ 3

2. Find the sentence which paraphrases "Individuals act to make themselves as well off as possible."

   _____
   _____

☞ 4

3. Classify the items in the Word Bank into Group A or Group B based on the type of utility. What do you think is the biggest difference between the two groups? Use key words and complete the sentence.

   Word Bank
   sports cars   French wines   concern for the environment
   caring about the fate of the Bengal tiger   homes   jobs   clean water
   birthday cakes for dogs

19

• LESSON 2 •

Group A	Group B
sports cars	concern for the environment

Key Words

materialistic   selfless   socially beneficial   self-centered

Group A is a set of _____ things, while Group B is more _____.

☞ 5

4. Why is the following question "nettlesome?":
   "Is it fair for those of us who live comfortably to impose our preferences on individuals in the developing world?"
   It is nettlesome because _____
   _____

5. Find the sentence which expresses the same idea as "I would sharpen my ax and start chopping."
   _____

☞ 6

6. Find the sentence which states the most important idea in the paragraph.
   _____

☞ 7-8

7. What is the "other important point regarding our individual preferences?"
   _____

8. Through what did Ms. McCarty maximize her utility?
   She had maximized her own utility not by _____
   _____, but by _____.

LISTENING: Economics

Before You Listen

If you had money to buy stocks and shares, in which domestic or international companies would you like to invest?

Word Focus

What words or expressions can you think of that are important to economics? Write **6 words** you learned from your research and their **definition**.

consumer (n.)	a person who buys goods and services for personal use

Listening 1: Short Summary

Listen to the passage and complete this summary of the listening using the following words in their correct forms (use 4 of the 5 words).

resource (n.)   society (n.)   borrow (v.)   distribute (v.)   produce (v.)

• LESSON 2 •

Economics is the study of how _____ use scarce _____ to _____ valuable commodities and _____ them among different people.

🎧 Listening 2: Question & Answer

Listen again to the passage and answer the following questions. You can use the box below to write notes.

1. In addition to steel, aluminum, plastics, glass and rubber, which other two resources are important in the production of cars?
   _____

2. Which two markets exist for the car industry?
   _____

3. Why is efficiency something important to consider in economics?
   _____

4. What did the lecture cost the students?
   _____

5. Why does the speaker think studying economics can be advantageous?
   _____

Notes

 True / False

Using your notes, discuss with your partner whether the following statements are true or false. Circle the correct answer and explain your decision.

1. Economics is about the production of goods, the resources used to make goods, and the distribution of goods.   True False
2. Efficiency is about accomplishing something with the least cost.   True False
3. Some resources are limited and some are unlimited.   True False
4. Economics is often regarded as a dismal subject.   True False
5. Studying economics has few practical benefits.   True False

DISCUSSION

If you could afford it, what could be your first "selfless" utility? Explain why it could make you happy.

A STEP FORWARD

Look up the term shown below and write what it means in your own words.

    limited government

FURTHER READING

［1］ベッカー、G. S. & R. A. ポズナー（2011）。『ベッカー教授、ポズナー判事の常識破りの経済学』鞍谷雅敏・遠藤幸彦・稲田誠士訳、東洋経済新報社。
［2］マンキュー、N. G.（2013）。『マンキュー経済学Ⅰミクロ編』（第3版）足立英之・石川城太・小川英治・地主敏樹・中馬宏之・柳川隆訳、東洋経済新報社。
［3］マンキュー、N. G.（2014）。『マンキュー経済学Ⅱマクロ編』（第3版）足立英之・石川城太・小川英治・地主敏樹・中馬宏之・柳川隆訳、東洋経済新報社。

［1］は、ノーベル経済学賞受賞者のゲイリー・ベッカーと法学者で連邦巡回区控訴裁判所判事でもあるリチャード・ポズナーが共同で運営したブログの記事を書籍化したものの続編で

ある。原著タイトル（*Uncommon Sense: Economic Insights, from Marriage to Terrorism*）にあるように結婚からテロまで幅広く経済学的に分析している。[2]と[3]は、経済学の入門書であり、世界中の大学で採用されている。言葉による説明と図や表が多く用いられており、必要とされる数学のレベルは中等教育程度である。経済学を体系的に学ぶ出発点として薦める。原書では2015年に第7版が出版された。

LESSON 3 What Is Natural Selection?

INTRODUCTION

　地球の歴史上で生物は進化を繰り返してきたと考えられています。具体的な例を挙げると恐竜が絶滅する前後に鳥類が繁栄しており、恐竜から鳥類へと進化の過程を彷彿させる始祖鳥が存在したことが近年明らかとなっています。また、現代人（ホモサピエンス）も約700万年前にアフリカ大陸を中心として活動していたアウストラロピテクスから進化したと言われています。こ

れは、姿・かたち（形態）が大きく変化したあるいは体の一部が大きくなった等、いわゆる形質の変化が証拠となっています。このことを我々は進化と一般に捉えています。このような形質の変化を観察し、進化がどのようにして生じたのかを説いた人物こそがチャールズ・ダーウィンです。ダーウィンは1859年に発刊した著書『種の起源』（*On the Origin of Species by Means of Natural Selection, or the Preservation of Favoured Races in the Struggle for Life*）において、このレッスンの英文で述べられていることを論理的に説明し世の中を驚かせました。この背景として、ダーウィンが進化論を提唱した19世紀半ばは西洋ではキリスト教の「創造論」が当たり前とされており、この世の万物は「神」が創造したものという概念が主流だったことが挙げられます。これらの背景により、進化論（自然選択説）は発表と同時に受け入れられるものではありませんでしたが、今日の進化生物学の発展に大きく寄与しています。

AIM & OBJECTIVE

CONTENT

　地球上に存在する生物は、驚くほど多様な姿・かたちをしています。いったいどのようにして、そのような多様性がもたらされているのでしょうか。ダーウィンが提唱した進化論は、生物の姿に対する人々の理解を大きく変えるものでした。このレッスンの英文では、自然選択（natural selection）や適応（adaptation）という概念を中心にダーウィンの考え方が紹介され、また生物の進化について誤解しがちな点についても書かれています。

LANGUAGE

　英文には文と文の結束性をもたせるためにいろいろな指示表現が多く用いられます。指示

表現が指すものを文脈から正確に把握しながら、英文を論理的に読んでみましょう。また、リスニングではこのレッスンのトピックに関する講義を聞き、内容理解や要約などの訓練を行います。

READING: What Evolution Did for Us

 ▶05

◆ Key Words & Phrases

natural selection	自然選択説。生物の種は多産性を原則とし、生存競争のために環境によく適応したものが子孫を残してその変異を伝える確率が高くなるという、進化論の根幹をなす理論。生物がもつ性質が3つの条件である「変異」(生物の個体には様々な変異が見られること)「遺伝」(変異の中には親から子へ伝えられるものがあること)「適応(選択)」(変異の中には自身の生存確率や次世代に残せる子孫の数に差を与えるものがあること)を満たすとき、生物集団の伝達的性質が変化する。
evolutionary biology	進化生物学。生物学の一分野で、共通祖先からの種の起源や進化、繁殖、生物多様性などについて研究を行う。
group selection	群(集団)選択説。生物の進化に関する理論の一つで、生物は種の保存や維持、利益や繁栄のために行動し、その解剖学的構造や行動はそのために都合よくできているという考え方。これに対して、individual selection(個体選択説)とは、個体の適応度の差が自然選択に有利に働くという考え方である。

[1]　When Darwin first developed his theory, people assumed that animals behaved in ways that were good for the species as a whole. For example, female lionesses which suckled young cubs belonging to other females in their pride were assumed to be doing so in order to make sure that there were plenty of lions in the next generation and so the species wouldn't become extinct. However, the [5] most important thing to note about the theory of natural selection is that it is concerned with *individual* survival and not with the survival of the species. Although individual reproduction inevitably has the effect of perpetuating species, this in itself is not the purpose of reproduction (or evolution).

出典：Dunbar, Robin, Louise Barrett & John Lycett. 2005. *Evolutionary Psychology: A Beginner's Guide*. London: Oneworld Publications. pp. 15–17. チャールズ・ダーウィンの「種の起源」の中でも、特に進化論について分かりやすく解説した入門書である。
[3]　**suckle**「授乳させる」
[3]　**cub**「(動物の)子供」
[4]　**make sure that ...**「…になるのを確実にする」
[8]　**reproduction**「生殖、繁殖」
[8]　**perpetuate**「永続させる」

2. Individuals are selected to behave in their own reproductive interests and the fate of the species as a whole is irrelevant to individuals' reproductive decisions. This must obviously be the case if natural selection is to operate in the way Darwin envisaged: since the whole process is based on the notion of inter-individual competition, any organism that behaves so as to benefit the species or group at some cost to its own reproductive interests is likely to leave fewer descendants than less noble-spirited individuals who just look after themselves.

3. So how did Darwin envisage natural selection as operating? While his views on the importance of natural selection in the evolutionary process changed over the course of his lifetime and evolutionary biologists today continue to argue over the relative importance of selection as a means of evolutionary change, there is no doubt whatsoever that, with this idea, Darwin changed forever the way we think about the natural world.

4. The theory of natural selection is deceptively simple and is based on three premises and their logical conclusion:

Premise 1: All individuals of a particular species show variation in their behavioural, morphological and/or physiological traits (their *phenotype*). This is usually known as the *Principle of Variation*.

Premise 2: A part of this variation between individuals is *heritable*: that is, some of that variation will be passed on from one generation to the next (or to put it even more simply, offspring will tend to resemble their parents more than they do other individuals in the population)—the *Principle of Inheritance*.

Premise 3: Whenever there is competition among individuals for scarce resources

---

[3] **this is the case if...** 「もし…であればこれは正しい、当然である」
[4] **envisage** 「(考えなど) を描く、把握する、想定する」
[5] **organism** 「動物や植物等の生命体」
[6] **at some cost to...** 「…を犠牲にして」
[7] **descendant** 「子孫」
[7] **noble-spirited** 「気概のある、高潔な」
[12] **whatsoever** no を伴う名詞の後で用いられると否定の意味を強調する。
[14] **deceptively** 「一見すると (実際と違って)」
[15] **premise** 「結論 (conclusion) を導き出すための基礎となる前提」
[17] **behavioural** 「行動に関する」本文中の名詞形の behaviour もイギリス英語の綴りで、アメリカ英語では behavior/behavioral となる。
[17] **morphological** 「形態的な」
[17] **physiological** 「生理的な」
[17] **trait** 「形質」生物がもつ性質や特徴のこと。
[17] **phenotype** 「表現型」
[19] **heritable** 「遺伝性の、遺伝する」
[20] **to put it even more simply** 「もっと分かりやすく言えば」
[21] **offspring** 「(人・動物の) 子供」

such as food, mates and somewhere to live, some of these variations will allow <u>their bearers</u> to compete more effectively than others. This competition occurs because organisms have a capacity to greatly increase in numbers and produce far more offspring than can ever give rise to breeding individuals (just think of frogspawn, for example)—the *Principle of Adaptation*.

Consequence: As a result of being more effective competitors, some individuals will leave more offspring than others, because the particular traits they possess give them some sort of edge: they are more successful at finding food, or mating, or avoiding predators. The offspring of <u>such individuals</u> will inherit these successful traits from their parents and 'natural selection' can be said to have taken place. Through this process, organisms become adapted to their environment. The success with which a trait is propagated in future generations, relative to other variants of that trait, is called its *fitness*. Fitness is a measure of relative reproductive success (that is, relative to alternative variants of the same trait); strictly speaking, it is a property of traits. This is sometimes known as the *Principle of Evolution*.

5   By specifying a mechanism by which evolutionary change could be effected, it then became possible to formulate testable hypotheses aimed at explaining the anatomy and behaviour of organisms. If a trait was an adaptation, then it should show evidence of being well adapted to the purpose it was supposed to serve; and if it continued to confer a selective advantage on the organism that possessed it, then it should also help to increase the survival and reproductive success of those organisms relative to those that did not possess it (or which possessed inferior versions of it).

6   A second important consequence of Darwin's position was that it made 'group selection' (evolution for the benefit of the species) an extremely unlikely (though

---

[4]   **give rise to ...**　「…を生じさせる」
[5]   **frogspawn**　「カエルの卵」
[9]   **edge**　「強み」
[13] **propagate**　「伝わる」
[15] **fitness**　「適応度」生物学用語としては、有機体が特定の環境で生存し子孫を残すこと。
[18] **effect**　「結果として生じさせる」
[19] **hypothesis**　「仮説」hypothesesは複数形。自然現象や社会現象の観察や実験の事例から現象を説明し、あるいは法則を導き出すために設けられる基本的な仮定のこと。
[20] **anatomy**　「(生命体の) 生体構造や組織」
[21] **serve the purpose**「目的にかなう (適合する)」という表現に注意。
[22] **confer ... on ~**　「…を~に与える、贈る」

not entirely impossible) explanation for the evolution of anything. Despite this, group selection remained firmly ensconced in the public imagination. Indeed, even biologists often failed to appreciate this point and it was not until the 1960s that the concept of group selection was finally laid to rest. Evolutionary biologists have remained extremely cautious of mentioning group selection ever since. *(750 words)*

[2]　**ensconced**　「定着した」
[4]　**lay . . . to rest**　「(出来事など)を終わりにする、決着をつける」

• LESSON 3 •

◆ Pre-class Task

Read the passage above. Mark each sentence as T (True) or F (False).

☞ ①

1. One assumption that people commonly had when Darwin published his theory was that female lions give milk to young cubs of the other lions for the survival of species. (   )

☞ ②

2. According to Darwin, reproduction is closely related to the survival of the species. (   )

☞ ③

3. Today's evolutionary biologists deny the relative importance of natural selection in the evolutionary process. (   )

☞ ④

4. Natural selection takes place when some competitive individuals leave their offspring some successful traits. (   )

☞ ⑤

5. One important consequence of Darwin's theory is that understanding of the mechanism of evolutionary change helped to explain the anatomy and behaviour of organisms. (   )

☞ ⑥

6. According to Darwin's position, the concept of group selection cannot effectively explain evolution. (   )

◆ In-class Task

Warm-up

What other animal behaviours do you know that help themselves and the group? Discuss in pairs.

• What Is Natural Selection? •

☞ 1
1. What is the typical misunderstanding regarding reproduction in the theory of natural selection?

_____

☞ 2
2. Which individual is likely to leave more descendants in Darwin's theory of natural selection? Choose the correct answer between A) and B) and explain the author's reason.

   A) One who behaves to benefit the species at some cost to its own reproduction.
   B) One who just looks after him/herself.

_____
_____

☞ 3
3. Although Darwin changed his views on the importance of natural selection during his life, what is his obvious contribution?

_____

☞ 4
4. What do the following underlined phrases in this paragraph indicate?

   this variation: _____
   _____

   their bearers: _____
   _____

   such individuals: _____
   _____

5. Explain why competition among individuals occurs.

_____
_____

☞ 5
6. What type of organism is successful at survival and reproduction?

_____

31

• LESSON 3 •

☞ 6

7. What is the point of Darwin's theory that biologists could not recognize before the 1960s?

_____

_____

LISTENING: Evolutionary Science

Before You Listen

What words do you know that relate to this image?

List the words here:

_____

Word Focus

What words can you think of that are important to understanding evolutionary science? Write **6 words** connected to the topic and an **example sentence** using them.

evolution (n.)	The process of evolution explains how living creatures develop.

32

• What Is Natural Selection? •

Listening 1: Short Summary

Listen to the passage and complete this summary of the listening using the following words in their correct forms (use 4 of the 5 words).

record (n.)   understand (v.)   hypothesis (n.)   evolution (n.)   test (v.)

The scientific method requires a _____ and a way to _____ it, and the fossil _____ is one example of how to demonstrate the scientific theory of _____.

Listening 2: Question & Answer

Listen again to the passage and answer the following questions. You can use the box below to write notes.

1. What are the two things the speaker says the scientific method helps to do?
   _____

2. What does the speaker say that you must collect and find before you make a hypothesis?
   _____

3. How does the speaker define 'fossils?'
   _____

4. According to the speaker, what findings strengthen the theory of evolution?
   _____

5. According to the speaker, how did some people react to Darwin's theories when they were first published?
   _____

Notes

• LESSON 3 •

 **True / False**

Using your notes, discuss with your partner whether the following statements are true or false. Circle the correct answer and explain your decision.

1. The speaker recommends changing your data to match your hypothesis. — True False
2. The speaker says that gaps in the fossil record are important in science. — True False
3. The speaker thinks that students should use the scientific method only when studying science. — True False
4. According to the speaker, being wrong is a positive thing. — True False
5. Today, most scientists agree with Darwin's theories. — True False

DISCUSSION

Based on Darwin's theory of evolution, try to come up with possible explanations to the following questions.

Why do giraffes have a long neck?

_____

_____

Why do male peacocks have large and colorful feathers?

_____

_____

Why do humans sometimes help others?

_____

_____

A STEP FORWARD

Research online about the following terms and write a short summary.

reciprocal altruism

_____

_____

inclusive fitness

_____

_____

FURTHER READING

［1］ブラウン、ジャネット（2007）。『ダーウィンの「種の起源」』（名著誕生2）長谷川眞理子訳、ポプラ社。
［2］Darwin, Charles（1859）. *On the Origin of Species*. London: John Murray.（邦訳：渡辺政隆訳『種の起源』（上下巻）光文社）
［3］栗田子郎（2013）。『進化生物学入門―宇宙発生からヒト誕生への137億年』講談社。
［4］宮田隆（2014）。『分子からみた生物進化―DNAが明かす生物の歴史』講談社。
［5］鈴木孝監修、数研出版編集部編（2014）。『視覚でとらえるフォトサイエンス生物図録』（改訂版）数研出版。

［1］はダーウィンが「種の起源」を書いた経緯から当時の賛否、そして現代の進化論までを網羅した1冊である。進化論の概観を簡単に学ぶことに適している。［2］はダーウィンの原著である。興味があれば、文理問わず在学中に一度原著を読むことをお薦めしたい。［3］は進化生物学を基礎から学べる1冊である。［4］はダーウィンが提唱した「種の起源」から現代の進化学までの流れが分かりやすく書かれた本であるので、大学の専門課程に進むまでに一度読んでおくことをお薦めしたい。［5］は高校生物履修時に副読本として手にした方も多いと考えられる。本図録中にはダーウィンの進化論だけでなく、他の学説が平易に書かれている。進化論の概要を押さえたい方には必携の本である。

LESSON 4 Power in World Politics

INTRODUCTION

　国際政治においてパワー（権力）は最も重要な概念の一つです。国際関係においては、国家の行動を強制する国際機関が存在しません。世界警察のようなものは存在しないので、国家間の争いは、当事者が同意しなければ国際司法裁判所で裁定を下すことはできないのです。このような世界では、自らのもつ軍事力などのパワーによって、各国は、自国が望む結果が実現されるよう相手国に対して行動することになります。

　国際政治の世界では、軍事力のように直接に他国を威圧しコントロールするパワーや、経済力のように直接他国に利益を与えることを通じて自国の望む行動をとらせるパワー（Hard Power）が強調されてきました。しかし他方で、情報が即座にグローバルな規模で伝達され、文化や政治的価値観が大きく広範な影響力をもつ現在、そういったものが他国を惹きつけ、自国の望む結果を実現させるある種のパワーとなりうるという考えがあります。これは「ソフト・パワー（Soft Power）」と呼ばれ、国際政治の重要な要素となっています。

AIM & OBJECTIVE

CONTENT

　このレッスンでは、国際政治の舞台で「ソフト・パワー」がもたらす作用について考えます。私たちがふだん、政治的意識をもたずに接している様々な国の文化や制度も「ソフト・パワー」の概念を用いて捉えると非常に有力な外交政策の一部となりうることが分かります。

LANGUAGE

　文章中に登場する具体例に注目します。例示（具体例の提示）がもつ役割を理解することで、その前後に述べられている抽象的な概念を正確に把握できるようになります。また、リスニングではこのレッスンのトピックに関する講義を聞き、内容理解や要約などの訓練を行います。

READING: Soft Power

◆ Key Words & Phrases

focus group	フォーカスグループとは、新製品や政治問題などに対する一般の反応を予測するために、司会者のもとに集団で討議（group interview）してもらう少人数からなる消費者などのグループのこと。
authoritarian	権威主義的な。非民主主義的な体制の一つとして、特定の指導者、政権が権力を独占する政治体制を指す。
spectrum	一連のもの（の範囲）、変域。両極の間のどのあたりに存在するかを示すのに使われる。
realist	国際政治学の分野では、以下のような点を強調して主張する研究者をリアリストという：① 国家が国際政治における主たる行為者（アクター）である、② 国家は「国益（ナショナル・インタレスト）」を追求する合理的な存在である、③ 国家は「国益」を実現する手段として、パワーを重視する、④ 国家より上位の権力が存在しない国際政治では、軍事・安全保障が最も重要な課題となる。

1. Everyone is familiar with hard power. We know that military and economic might often get others to change their position. Hard power can rest on inducements ("carrots") or threats ("sticks"). But sometimes you can get the outcomes you want without tangible threats or payoffs. The indirect way to get what you want has sometimes been called "the second face of power." A country may obtain the outcomes it wants in world politics because other countries—admiring its values, emulating its example, aspiring to its level of prosperity and openness—want to follow it. In this sense, it is also important to set the agenda and attract others in world politics, and not only to force them to change by threatening military force or economic sanctions. This soft power—getting

---

出典：Nye, Joseph S., Jr. 2004. *Soft Power: The Means to Success in World Politics.* New York: Public Affairs. pp. 5–8.（邦訳：山岡洋一訳『ソフト・パワー——21世紀国際政治を制する見えざる力』日本経済新聞社）著者ジョセフ・ナイは国際政治学を代表するアメリカの学者であり、本著は彼が提唱した「ソフト・パワー」という概念についての議論を総括、整理したもの。国際政治の新たな枠組みを提示した1冊として高く評価されている。

[2] **rest on ...**「…に基づく、依存している」
[3] **inducement**「誘因」
[4] **payoff**「報酬」
[5] **the second face of power**「（権力の）第二の顔」権力にはものごとを決定するという積極的な側面と、紛争などを表面化させず潜在的な争点を握りつぶす「非決定」という側面があるとされる。ここでの「第二の顔」とは後者を指す。
[8] **agenda**「計画」実施すべき手順を具体的に記したものを指す。
[10] **sanction**「（国際法違反などに対する）制裁」

others to want the outcomes that you want—co-opts people rather than coerces them.

2. Soft power rests on the ability to shape the preferences of others. At the personal level, we are all familiar with the power of attraction and seduction. In a relationship or a marriage, power does not necessarily reside with the larger partner, but in the mysterious chemistry of attraction. And in the business world, smart executives know that leadership is not just a matter of issuing commands, but also involves leading by example and attracting others to do what you want. It is difficult to run a large organization by commands alone. You also need to get others to buy into your values. Similarly, contemporary practices of community-based policing rely on making the police sufficiently friendly and attractive that a community wants to help them achieve shared objectives.

3. Political leaders have long understood the power that comes from attraction. If I can get you to want to do what I want, then I do not have to use carrots or sticks to make you do it. Whereas leaders in authoritarian countries can use coercion and issue commands, politicians in democracies have to rely more on a combination of inducement and attraction. Soft power is a staple of daily democratic politics. The ability to establish preferences tends to be associated with intangible assets such as an attractive personality, culture, political values and institutions, and policies that are seen as legitimate or having moral authority. If a leader represents values that others want to follow, it will cost less to lead.

4. Soft power is not merely the same as influence. After all, influence can also rest on the hard power of threats or payments. And soft power is more than just persuasion or the ability to move people by argument, though that is an important part of it. It is also the ability to attract, and attraction often leads to acquiescence. Simply put, in behavioral terms soft power is attractive power. In terms of

---

[1] **co-opt** 「(団体・運動等に)(反対者・少数グループ)を吸収する、取り込む」
[1] **coerce** 「強制する、(暴力や権威などによって)抑制する、抑圧する」
[3] **preference** 「好み、好みについて行われる選択、選好」
[4] **attraction** 「魅力、惹きつける力」
[4] **seduction** 「誘惑」
[10] **buy into ...** 「(考えなど)を受け入れる、信じる」
[12] **shared objective** 「共通の目的」
[17] **staple** 「中心的なもの、欠かせないもの」
[19] **asset** 「交換価値のある所有物、強み」
[26] **acquiescence** 「黙従、黙認」
[27] **in behavioral terms** 「行動学的な点から見ると」in ... terms または in terms of ... は「...の点から見ると」という意味のイディオム。

resources, soft-power resources are the assets that produce such attraction. Whether a particular asset is a soft-power resource that produces attraction can be measured by asking people through polls or focus groups. Whether that attraction in turn produces desired policy outcomes has to be judged in particular cases. Attraction does not always determine others' preferences, but this gap between power measured as resources and power judged as the outcomes of behavior is not unique to soft power. It occurs with all forms of power. Before the fall of France in 1940, Britain and France had more tanks than Germany, but that advantage in military power resources did not accurately predict the outcome of the battle.

5 One way to think about the difference between hard and soft power is to consider the variety of ways you can obtain the outcomes you want. You can command me to change my preferences and do what you want by threatening me with force or economic sanctions. You can induce me to do what you want by using your economic power to pay me. You can restrict my preferences by setting the agenda in such a way that my more extravagant wishes seem too unrealistic to pursue. Or you can appeal to my sense of attraction, love, or duty in our relationship and appeal to our shared values about the justness of contributing to those shared values and purposes. If I am persuaded to go along with your purposes without any explicit threat or exchange taking place—in short, if my behavior is determined by an observable but intangible attraction—soft power is at work. Soft power uses a different type of currency (not force, not money) to engender cooperation—an attraction to shared values and the justness and duty of contributing to the achievement of those values. Much as Adam Smith observed that people are led by an invisible hand when making decisions in a free market, our decisions in the marketplace for ideas are often shaped by soft power—an intangible attraction that persuades us to go along with others' purposes without any explicit threat or exchange taking place.

---

[4]　**in turn**　「順繰りに、順を追って」
[8]　**the fall of France in 1940**　「(ナチス・ドイツの) 1940年のフランス侵攻」ドイツ軍を始めとする枢軸軍と連合軍の戦闘。これによりドイツ軍は連合国軍に駆逐される1944年までフランスを占領した。また1940–41年の間、ドイツ軍はイギリスに対しても大規模な空襲を行った。
[16]　**extravagant**　「度を超した、途方もない」
[23]　**engender**　「生む、引き起こす」
[24]　**much as ...**　「…だけれども」even though とほぼ同義である。
[25]　**Adam Smith**　スコットランドの哲学者・経済学者 (1723–90)。『国富論』(1776) を著した古典派経済学の祖として知られる。

6. Hard and soft power are related because they are both aspects of the ability to achieve one's purpose by affecting the behavior of others. The distinction between them is one of degree, both in the nature of the behavior and in the tangibility of the resources. Command power—the ability to change what others do—can rest on coercion or inducement. Co-optive power—the ability to shape what others want—can rest on the attractiveness of one's culture and values or the ability to manipulate the agenda of political choices in a manner that makes others fail to express some preferences because they seem to be too unrealistic. The types of behavior between command and co-option range along a spectrum from coercion to economic inducement to agenda setting to pure attraction. Soft-power resources tend to be associated with the co-optive end of the spectrum of behavior, whereas hard-power resources are usually associated with command behavior. But the relationship is imperfect. For example, sometimes countries may be attracted to others with command power by myths of invincibility, and command power may sometimes be used to establish institutions that later become regarded as legitimate. A strong economy not only provides resources for sanctions and payments, but can also be a source of attractiveness. On the whole, however, the general association between the types of behavior and certain resources is strong enough to allow us to employ the useful shorthand reference to hard- and soft-power resources.

7. In international politics, the resources that produce soft power arise in large part from the values an organization or country expresses in its culture, in the examples it sets by its internal practices and policies, and in the way it handles its relations with others. Governments sometimes find it difficult to control and employ soft power, but that does not diminish its importance. It was a former French foreign minister who observed that the Americans are powerful because they can "inspire the dreams and desires of others, thanks to the mastery of global images through film and television and because, for these same reasons, large numbers of students from other countries come to the United States to finish their studies." Soft power is an important reality. Even the great British realist E. H. Carr, writing in 1939, described international power in three categories: military, economic, and power over opinion. Those who deny the importance of soft power are like people who do not understand the power of seduction. *(1233 words)*

---

[15] **invincibility**　「無敵であること」
[19] **employ the shorthand reference to ...**　「とりあえず簡潔に…へと関連づける」
[31] **E. H. Carr**　イギリスの歴史家・政治学者・外交官 (1892–1982)。国際関係学の研究者として知られる。

• Power in World Politics •

◆ Pre-class Task

Read the passage above. Mark each sentence as T (True) or F (False).

☞ ①
1. Economic sanctions are an example of hard power. (　　)

☞ ③
2. "Carrots" and "sticks" are both effective uses of soft power. (　　)
3. Soft power is effective when it reflects values that others are likely to follow. (　　)

☞ ④
4. The assets to generate attraction are called soft-power resources. (　　)

☞ ⑤
5. In this paragraph, the word "currency" means "resources invested to affect the behavior of others." (　　)

☞ ⑦
6. Governments sometimes struggle to control and employ soft power effectively. (　　)
7. The significance of soft power has not been recognized. (　　)

◆ In-class Task

Warm-up

Work in pairs. What is "Soft Power" in your everyday life? Suggest at least two concrete examples of how to use soft power successfully in your everyday life.

Reading Comprehension

☞ ①
1. A) Find the examples of "inducements" and "threats" in this paragraph.
   B) Why does the author use those examples?
   A) inducements: _____　threats: _____
   B) _____
   _____

• LESSON 4 •

☞ 2

2. What can be "soft power" in our daily lives? Find two examples in this paragraph.
   _____
   _____

☞ 3

3. What are "intangible assets" used for establishing preferences? Find the examples from this paragraph.
   _____

☞ 4

4. Which country held a dominant position in the battle in 1940?
   _____

☞ 5

5. Find a synonym and two antonyms for "invisible" in this paragraph.
   Synonym: _____   Antonyms: _____

☞ 6

6. Choose the correct term from the box to fill in each blank in the diagram shown below.

   attraction   coercion   co-opt   inducement

Hard	Soft
( ) ( )	agenda setting ( )
←——+————+————	————+————+——→
Command	( )

☞ 7

7. What is the former French foreign minister's observation of the U.S.?
   the U.S. soft power resources: _____
   Outcome: _____

• Power in World Politics •

LISTENING: Power in Politics

 ▶08

Before You Listen

In 2004, a young and unknown Barack Obama gave the speech of his life at a large political gathering in Boston. As a result of his success and appeal, he suddenly became a leading contender in the 2008 presidential campaign.

Clearly, speeches, debates on TV, and interviews in the media are extremely important in American politics, but what about in Japan and the rest of the world?

Word Focus

What words or expressions can you think of that are important in politics? Write **6 words** you learned from your research and an **example** of how they are connected to your life.

election (n.)	The 2016 presidential election.

43

• LESSON 4 •

🎧 Listening 1: Short Summary

Listen to the passage and complete this summary of the listening using the following words in their correct forms (use 4 of the 5 words).

| benefit (n.) | classify (v.) | power (n.) | subtract (v.) | relationship (n.) |

_____ in politics and human _____ is about creating _____, and according to Bertrand Russell it can be _____ into three basic types: 1) physical power, 2) power through rewards and punishments, and 3) power to influence opinion.

🎧 Listening 2: Question & Answer

Listen again to the passage and answer the following questions. You can use the box below to write notes.

1. What aggressive act of physical power took place in 1939?

2. How can SEZs help foreign investors?

3. Which country started to set up SEZs in the early 1980s?

4. How can economic sanctions affect trade between countries?

5. Why is communicative intelligence especially important for today's politicians?

Notes

 **True / False**

Using your notes, discuss with your partner whether the following statements are true or false. Circle the correct answer and explain your decision.

1. All students must attend the debating seminar. True False
2. When Poland invaded Germany, it was an act of physical power. True False
3. SEZs are created for economic reasons. True False
4. Sanctions are used to persuade other countries to act differently. True False
5. Bertrand Russell's "power to influence opinion" comes close to Joseph Nye's definition of soft power. True False

DISCUSSION

What do you think Japan's soft power resources are? Make a list, and discuss what you expect to be the results of using these powers.

___

A STEP FORWARD

Look up the following words and write explanations with examples by yourself.

cool Britannia

___

cultural diplomacy

___

FURTHER READING

[1] ナイ、ジョセフ S. ジュニア & デイヴィッド A. ウェルチ（2013）。『国際紛争——理論と歴史』（原書第9版）田中明彦・村田晃嗣訳、有斐閣。

［2］カー、E. H.（2011）。『危機の二十年—理想と現実』原彬久訳、岩波書店。
［3］芝崎厚士（2015）。「そふと・ぱわあ考—国際関係現象としての国際関係研究」同『国際関係の思想史—グローバル関係研究のために』所収、147–210、岩波書店。
［4］マッグレイ、ダグラス（2003）。「ナショナルクールという新たな国力—世界を闊歩する日本のカッコよさ」『中央公論』第118巻第5号、130–140、中央公論新社。

［1］はリーディングテキストの著者ナイと新たに共著者に加わったウェルチによる国際関係の書。ハーヴァード大学における講義をもとにしており、各国の大学の国際関係論の講義で広く用いられている。［2］は国際関係論の古典である。イギリスの国際政治学者・歴史家であるE. H. カーは、本書において1930年代に支配的であった国際法や国際世論を重視する議論をユートピアニズムと呼び、その目的論的思考を批判する。その上で、国際政治におけるパワーを重視する思考（リアリズム）に立脚し、理想や道義の実現を目指すことを主張している。［3］は国際関係とは何かを問う論稿であり、その具体的な分析対象としてナイの「ソフト・パワー」を取り上げている。ここでは、この概念が提起され、変化していく過程をたどるとともに、「ソフト・パワー」がどのように使用されているかを考察している。［4］は日本の「クール・ジャパン」という言葉、戦略の由来となったとされる論文である。小論であるが、「ソフト・パワー」という言葉に言及して日本文化を論じた嚆矢と位置づけられる論稿である。マッグレイは、ファッション、アニメ、料理、ポップミュージックなど幅広い分野で、日本の国際的な文化影響力は静かに成長し、すでに潜在的な「ソフト・パワー」を有していると論じた。

LESSON 5
Intelligent Transportation Systems

INTRODUCTION

　交通事故の約90％は人的要因によるものと言われています。そのため、交通安全対策においては運転者や歩行者等の道路利用者の人的エラーを取り除くことが重要です。近年では、高度道路交通システム（ITS: Intelligent Transportation Systems）など、情報通信技術を利用して交通安全対策を始めとする道路交通における問題を解決するための研究が盛んになってきました。車両には数十個のセンサーが搭載され、車速や現在位置など様々な情報を測定し、運転支援や車両制御が行われています。道路上や道路周辺のインフラ設備にもセンサーや通信機器が設置され、車両と車両が通信する車車間通信や車両とインフラ設備が通信する路車間通信によって、運転者への安全運転支援や情報提供が行えるようになってきています。また、車両の運転動作を完全に自動化する自動運転システムも高速道路でのテストが実施されるなど、実用化に向けた研究・開発が盛んになってきています。

AIM & OBJECTIVE

CONTENT
　高度道路交通システムを使用した運転者への情報提供、予防安全、事故防止システムなどについて理解を深めます。これらの自動化されたシステムには、運転者の人的エラーの回避に有効な側面と課題の両側面があることが分かっています。

LANGUAGE
　前後の文の繋がりを円滑にするために主語と動詞の順番が入れ替わることがあります。こうした文のことを倒置構文（inversion or inverted sentence）と呼びます。英文の中から倒置構文を見つけ出し、その文体的特徴と英文を読む場合の効果を理解しましょう。また、リスニングではこのレッスンのトピックに関する講義を聞き、内容理解や要約などの訓練を行います。

• LESSON 5 •

READING: Driving Vehicles of the Future

 ▶09

◆ Key Words & Phrases

Intelligent Transportation Systems (ITS)	高度道路交通システム。道路交通の安全性、輸送効率、快適性の向上等を目的に、最先端の情報通信技術等を用いて、人と道路と車両とを一体のシステムとして構築する新しい道路交通システムの総称。
adaptive cruise control (ACC)	定速走行・車間距離制御装置、車間距離制御システム。前方車両との車間距離をレーダーなどで計測し、車両の速度を自動制御することで一定の車間距離を保つシステム。
smart sign	スマート・サイン。車のフロントガラス上に表示される危険の警告や規制情報など。
vision enhancement systems (VES)	視覚強化システム。夜間や雨天時などにおいて、運転者の視界を補助するためのシステムの総称。
External Vehicle Speed Control (EVSC)	外部車速コントロール。車両が走行している場所や環境に応じて車両の最高速度を制御するシステム。
LCD screen	液晶ディスプレイスクリーン（LCD は *l*iquid *c*rystal *d*isplay の略）。車両用にはカーナビゲーションシステムや、車両後方を確認するためのバックカメラの表示装置などに使われる。

1. Future vehicles can be expected to present a good deal of information, especially inside vehicles, using Intelligent Transportation Systems or ITS. Their use reflects the general philosophy that safety problems can be remedied with new technology. Availability of technology, rather than driver information needs, appears to be driving the industry to add many of these features to new vehicles. [5] However, our understanding of human abilities has not kept up with the rapid advances in vehicle technology. Use of such systems will be a challenge for many older drivers. Among the ITS that are already available or being developed are:
   - in-vehicle navigation systems that tell a driver's location, directions to a destination, alternate routes, location of congestion or accidents, when to turn [10] at intersections, names of upcoming streets, and more

出典：Dewar, Robert & Paul Olson. 2007. *Human Factors in Traffic Safety*. Tucson: Lawyers & Judges Publishing Company. pp. 287–289. 交通事故の主要な原因である人的要因について、道路利用者の行動を中心とした幅広い解説がなされている。交通事故の調査や交通安全の推進を行う人にとって有用な情報が多く紹介されている。

[3] **remedy**　(v.)「改善する」
[11] **intersection**　「一般道路の交差点」高速道路の合流点は interchange.

48

- adaptive cruise control, where sensors detect the distance to the vehicle ahead and adjust speed so as to create a safe following distance
- "smart signs" project on the windscreen containing information warning of hazards (e.g., railroad crossing) or regulations (e.g., speed limit change); these could replace or supplement existing roadside signs
- collision warning systems, which let drivers know when they are closing in too fast on a fixed object or another vehicle (to prevent rear-end collisions, side swipe, and run-off-road accidents)
- crash avoidance systems that actually take control of the vehicle if a collision is otherwise inevitable
- vision enhancement systems (VES) that detect hazards such as pedestrians and animals on the road at night, allowing the driver to detect hazards that might otherwise be detected too late or not at all; other VES include ultraviolet headlights which reflect more light back from special pavement markings and hazards (bridge abutments) at night
- headlights that shine around curves as vehicles begin to turn, allowing vision farther ahead on curves
- information of interest to tourists (accommodation, fuel, food, and so forth) which now appears mainly on signs
- communication devices such as phones, e-mail, and fax machines
- additional vehicle systems monitoring, some of which may not be necessary (e.g., outside temperature)
- emergency alerting systems meant to provide to a dispatch center emergency information about breakdowns, accidents, and other events that require assistance (e.g., ambulance, tow truck); such alerting devices give an increased sense of security to drivers.

2 It is also possible in the future to have devices in vehicles which communicate driver actions and condition, vehicle location, speed, and maneuvers to a central processing station for recording. This would be accomplished with sensors and transmitters in vehicles and in or beside the road.

---

[3] **windscreen** 「(自動車の)フロントガラス」アメリカ英語では windshield.
[8] **side swipe** 「車の側面の接触」
[10] **otherwise** 「別のやり方で」
[15] **bridge abutment** 「橋台」
[23] **provide** 「供給する、提供する」provide...to ~「…を~に供給[提供]する」という語順が普通だが、本文では provide の直接目的語の記述が詳細で長いため語順が入れ替わっている。
[23] **dispatch center** 「ロードサービスセンター」
[25] **tow truck** 「レッカー車」
[28] **maneuver** 「運転操作」

3. As the workload, both physical and mental, increases in complex systems, designers have introduced automation to reduce the load. This is the case with motor vehicles in which we now see automatic gear shifting, power steering, cruise control, and so on. With increased automation, and an apparently "easier" driving task, comes a shift in the driver's role from operational to supervisory, raising concerns about inattention and reduced vigilance. Young and Stanton (1997) suggest that automated systems could reduce driver workload to such an extent that it may be detrimental to driving performance. Humans operate best at an optimal level of arousal, and either too much or too little workload can be detrimental to performance. One argument is that if vehicle operation becomes too automated (e.g., adaptive cruise control, steering which keeps the car in its lane until interrupted) drivers will reduce attention and gradually lose the ability to control the vehicle when it comes to an emergency in which they must take control. Real-life tasks involve a balance of automatic and controlled processes, and mental load is determined by the proportions of each.

4. Vehicle speed is an issue in many collisions; therefore there might be an advantage to having automated speed control. Among the systems that have been studied to control vehicle speed is the External Vehicle Speed Control (EVSC) being tested in the U.K. Intelligent speed adaptation devices detect the vehicle speed and provide feedback to drivers or limit vehicle speed. In the case of an "advisory" system the driver is informed of the speed limit and changes in the speed limit (e.g., through built-up areas). With a "voluntary" system the driver is able to disable the system, and in the "mandatory" mode the system limits the vehicle speed at all times. In addition, the speed limits can be fixed (the posted limit), variable (changed based on location, such as reduced near pedestrian crossings) or dynamic (e.g., modified by weather or traffic conditions). The best estimates of the accident savings vary from ten percent for a fixed advisory system to 36 percent for a mandatory dynamic system.

---

[1] **workload** 「作業負荷」
[2] **this is the case with ...** 「…に当てはまる」
[3] **automatic gear shifting** 「自動変速」
[3] **power steering** 「パワーステアリング」ハンドル操作を軽くするための油圧などによる舵取り装置。
[6] **vigilance** 「警戒心」
[6] Young, M. & N. Stanton (1997). "Taking the Load Off: Investigating the Effects of Vehicle Automation on Mental Workload." In S. A. Robertson (ed), *Contemporary Ergonomics*, pp. 98–103.
[7] **to such an extent that ...** 「…するほどまでに」
[8] **detrimental** 「支障をきたす」
[22] **built-up area** 「市街地、建物密集区域」
[27] **accident saving** 「交通事故減少率」

Estimates of reduction in fatal accidents are even higher (18 to 59 percent, respectively, for the two systems).

5. With the advancement in mobile office technology comes more opportunity for drivers to process information while on the move. The cognitive demands of a speech-based e-mail system were examined by Jamson et al. (2004). In a simulator study, incoming e-mails were either controlled by the system (the driver was alerted to the arrival of a message which was then presented by a voice system, displayed on an LCD screen in the center of the dashboard), or controlled by the driver (who was alerted but decided when to accept the message). Drivers were required to respond to the messages while driving. Performance was generally better—reduced time to detect a collision and reduced anticipation to braking demands—when the driver controlled e-mail reception, and drivers were less responsive when processing e-mails. This showed the "increased cognitive costs" associated with the decision making required of the driver.

6. Speech-based interface was also studied in a car-following task by Lee et al. (2001), who measured how a speech-based e-mail system influenced drivers' response to a lead vehicle which braked periodically. There was a 30 percent increase in reaction time when the speech-based system was used, as compared with a condition where the e-mail system was not used. Traffic density was also manipulated in this simulator study. Subjective workload ratings showed that speech-based interaction led to a significant workload which was highest for the complex e-mail system (with more menus and more options). The more complex driving environment also increased response time, but only when the system was used.

7. Behavioral adaptation is the tendency for drivers to modify their behavior to adjust to new conditions or modifications to the road, environment, or vehicle. Drivers typically slow in poor weather, increase attention in heavy traffic, and so

---

[5] Jamson, A. H., S. J. Westerman, G. R. J. Hockey & O. M. J. Carsten (2004). "Speech-based E-mail and Driver Behavior: Effects of an In-vehicle Message System Interface." *Human Factors* 46: 4. pp. 625–639.
[6] either ... or ~ の相関語句（ともに過去分詞）に注意。
[12] **anticipation** 「予測して反応する時間」
[16] **car-following task** 「追従走行タスク」定速走行制御などの実験で行われる。
[16] Lee, J. D., B. Caven, S. Haake & T. L. Brown (2001). "Speech-based Interaction with In-vehicle Computers: the Effects of Speech-based E-mail on Drivers' Attention to the Roadway." *Human Factors* 43. pp. 631–640.
[18] **periodically** 「定期的に」
[21] **subjective workload rating** 「主観的作業負荷評価」尺度得点を用いた作業負荷の評価方法。

on. But how will they respond to the presence of ITS in vehicles? Smiley (2000) provides a good review of the ITS that may affect driver adaptation behavior. Drivers who have vehicles with collision warning systems may speed or follow too closely. Adaptive cruise control (ACC) may reduce driver workload, leading to less time looking at the road or more time driving in heavy traffic when tired. ACC does not respond to stopped vehicles on the road, one of the most dangerous conditions leading to rear-end collisions.

8   Fully automated highways, which relieve the driver of the driving task, would seem to be an ideal solution to safety problems. However, a number of human factors issues arise when considering how this would operate. Drivers may become complacent about the driving task and not be paying attention when it came time to take control upon leaving an automated road, or if there were technical difficulties suddenly requiring them to take control of the vehicle. Many drivers would object to the loss of control, as steering, shifting gears, and accelerating play a major role in the "joy of driving." *(1261 words)*

---

[1] Smiley, A. (2000). "Behavioral Adaptation, Safety, and Intelligent Transportation Systems." *Transportation Research Record* #1724. pp. 47–51.
[9] **human factor** 「人的要因」
[11] **complacent** 「自己満足した」

● Intelligent Transportation Systems ●

◆ Pre-class Task
Read the passage above. Mark each sentence as T (True) or F (False).

☞ ①–②

1. The vehicle industry developed ITS because it is necessary for drivers. (   )

☞ ③

2. Complex driving systems will not increase the driver's workload. (   )

☞ ④

3. The advisory system of the EVSC is more likely to save fatal accidents than the mandatory system. (   )

☞ ⑤

4. In a simulator study of Jamson et al. (2004), cognitive demands on the drivers were lower when they were in control of e-mail reception. (   )

☞ ⑥

5. Both Lee et al. (2001) and Jamson et al. (2004) conducted studies on the speech-based e-mail system. (   )

☞ ⑦

6. In poor weather conditions or heavy traffic, drivers tend to adjust their behavior in response to the new situation. (   )

☞ ⑧

7. The author concludes that the fully automated highway that relieves the driver of the driving task is an ideal solution to safety problems. (   )

◆ In-class Task

● Warm-up

When you choose a car, which is your highest priority: speed, safety, comfort, controllability or something else? Share your opinion with your partner stating three reasons.

• LESSON 5 •

☞ 1

1. The author claims, "<u>Our understanding of human abilities has not kept up with the rapid advances in vehicle technology. Use of such systems will be a challenge for many older drivers</u>." Why do you think some of the systems listed in this paragraph would be a challenge for them?

___

☞ 3

2. According to Young and Stanton (1997), how could reduced driver workload be detrimental to driving performance?

___

☞ 4

3. How does the mandatory dynamic system of the EVSC automatically control vehicle speed?

___

☞ 5

4. The simulator study of Jamson et al. (2004) indicated that cognitive costs were increased when decision making was required of the driver. What evidence do they provide to support this claim?

___

☞ 6

5. According to the simulator study of Lee et al. (2001), what led to the increased driver's reaction time to the leading car?

___

• Intelligent Transportation Systems •

☞ 7

6. What is the difference in drivers' adaptation behavior between vehicles with ITS and vehicles without? Explain the differences using some examples.

   Vehicles without ITS: _____
   _____

   Vehicles with ITS: _____
   _____
   _____

☞ 8

7. Give two main examples describing "human factors issues" regarding ITS.
   _____
   _____

8. An inverted sentence is a sentence in which the predicate (verb) comes before the subject. In the following example,
   With the advancement in mobile office technology comes more opportunity for drivers to process information while on the move. (paragraph 5, line 1)
   the subject and the verb are inverted.

A) Rewrite this sentence as a sentence consisting of the subject followed by the verb.
   _____
   _____

B) Considering the context in paragraph 5, the inverted sentence is preferable to the sentence rewritten in A). Read paragraph 5 again and explain why.
   _____
   _____
   _____
   _____
   _____

C) There are three more inverted sentences in the following three paragraphs of this passage. Write down the first and the last word of those sentences.
   ⟨Paragraph 1⟩ first word: _____ ... last word: _____
   ⟨Paragraph 3⟩ first word: _____ ... last word: _____
   ⟨Paragraph 4⟩ first word: _____ ... last word: _____

• LESSON 5 •

LISTENING: Automation

 Before You Listen

Write a list of the automatic things in your daily life:

_____

_____

Word Focus

What words or expressions can you think of that are related to modern automatic devices? Write **6 words** related to the topic and an **example** of how they are connected to your life.

automation (n.)	The automation of train systems makes my journeys safer.

Listening 1: Short Summary

Listen to the passage and complete this summary of the listening using the following words in their correct forms (use 4 of the 5 words).

driver (n.)   convenient (adj.)   device (n.)   people (n.)   think (v.)

Modern life has many _____ products, but some _____ worry that we do not _____ enough about the effects of _____ becoming easier.

Listening 2: Question & Answer

Listen again to the passage and answer the following questions. You can use the box below to write notes.

1. According to the speaker, what do some people do while they are driving because they feel relaxed?
   _____
   _____

2. What is the significance of the number 3000?
   _____
   _____

3. Why does the speaker say modern day driving and eating are similar?
   _____
   _____

4. What are some other examples of common automation that the speaker mentions?
   _____
   _____

5. What does the speaker say about life being *too* convenient?
   _____
   _____

Notes

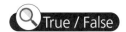 True / False

Using your notes, discuss with your partner whether the following statements are true or false. Circle the correct answer and explain your decision.

1. According to the speaker, automation is always bad. — True False

2. One of the side effects of having more technology in cars is drivers having more free time. — True False

3. The speaker suggests that younger drivers are less safe than older drivers. — True False

4. The speaker believes that more automation is better if one doesn't consider specific examples like driving. — True False

5. The speaker says that there are always negative consequences to living a convenient life. — True False

DISCUSSION

When driving, which of the ITS features described in paragraph 1 of the reading passage do you feel would be overly distracting?

A STEP FORWARD

Research online about how the following systems work and write a short summary.

telematics

_____

run-off-road protection

_____

FURTHER READING

[1] Barnard, Yvonne, Ralf Risser & Josef Krems (2011). *The Safety of Intelligent Driver Support Systems: Design, Evaluation and Social Perspectives.* Farnham: Ashgate.
[2] 蓮花一己・向井希宏（2012）。『交通心理学』（放送大学教材）放送大学教育振興会。

［3］杉浦孝明・佐藤雅明（2014）。『自動車ビッグデータでビジネスが変わる！―プローブカー最前線』インプレス R&D.
［4］ヴァンダービルト、トム（2008）。『となりの車線はなぜスイスイ進むのか？―交通の科学』酒井泰介訳、早川書房。
［5］ワイルド、ジェラルド J. S.（2007）。『交通事故はなぜなくならないか―リスク行動の心理学』芳賀繁訳、新曜社。

［1］はITSを用いた運転支援システムについて広い領域の観点から有効性や問題点などについて評価している。一部、専門的な内容を含むが、道路交通の領域を専門とする人には有益な情報が多く得られる書籍である。［2］は、人的要因（ヒューマンファクター）による事故発生のメカニズムやITS技術と交通心理学との関連などについて幅広く解説している。［3］は、車両に取りつけられたセンサーによってどのような情報を収集できるか、インターネットを介した他システムとの連携によってどのようなサービスが実現可能かについて解説している。［4］は交通安全の問題だけでなく交通場面で生じる様々な疑問について、交通心理学や交通工学の視点から解説している。著者はジャーナリストであり、交通管制官、自動車メーカー、保険会社など道路交通に関わる様々な職種の意見が取り込まれている。一般読者向けに出版されている書であるため、専門知識を必要としない内容となっている。［5］は交通安全について、リスク・ホメオスタシスという理論に基づき交通心理学・交通工学の立場から考察している。本文において、衝撃警告システムを搭載した車両の運転者はより高い速度で運転し前方車両に接近するとの一文がある。本書は、運転者がなぜそのような行動を取るのか、なぜ安全性を高める装置を搭載したのに事故が減らないのか、といったことについて理解を深める助けとなるだろう。

LESSON 6
Language and Thought

INTRODUCTION

「比喩（ひゆ）」（隠喩）と聞いてどのようなイメージをもつでしょうか。これはメタファーの一般的な訳語ですが、「君は僕の太陽だ」といった詩的な表現を思い浮かべる人が多いかもしれません。

確かにそのような一面もありますが、実はメタファーは私たちの思考のもっと深いところに関わっていると考えられています。次の表現を比べてみましょう。

1. The army attacked the town.
2. Some researchers attacked the weak points of his argument.

1は戦争等で軍隊が街に物理的な攻撃をしたことを表す文です。一方、2は物理的な「攻撃」ではなく、弁論で他者を非難するいわば「口撃」です。主張を attack するだけではなく、defend することもできます。また、議論に「勝つ（win）」ことも「負ける（lose）」こともできます。このように「戦争」と「議論」に関する表現には驚くべき類似性を見ることができます。このことは、私たちが「議論」を「戦争」に見立てて考えているということを示しています。言語学では「言葉」を観察することで、このような思考を形成するメタファーを見つける試みが行われています。言葉を研究することで、私たちが世界をどのように切り取り、理解しているかということが分かってきます。

AIM & OBJECTIVE

CONTENT

このレッスンでは「メタファー」について考えます。ふだん何気なく使っている言語ですが、意識的に観察してみるといろいろと興味深い発見があります。メタファーは認知言語学と呼ばれる分野で広く研究されていて、私たちの思考の基礎になるものだと考えられています。

LANGUAGE

言語のメタファー的な使用について学習します。メタファーを理解することで、英語の表現の成り立ちや意味をよく理解できるようになります。また、リスニングではこのレッスンのトピックに関する講義を聞き、内容理解や要約などの訓練を行います。

READING: Concepts We Live by

◆ Key Words & Phrases

rhetorical flourish	修辞上の飾り、言葉のあや。メタファーを表面的なものとして捉えていることを指す。
conceptual system	概念システム。物事の捉え方や考え方の体系を指す。
conceptual metaphor	概念メタファー。人間の思考に関わるメタファーを指す。A is B の形で表されることが多い。一般に抽象的な概念をより具体的な概念を通して理解する場合が多く、前者を target domain（目標領域）、後者を source domain（根源領域）と呼ぶ。前ページの例では「議論」が target domain,「戦争」が source domain となる。

1 Metaphor is for most people a device of the poetic imagination and the rhetorical flourish—a matter of extraordinary rather than ordinary language. Moreover, metaphor is typically viewed as characteristic of language alone, a matter of words rather than thought or action. For this reason, most people think they can get along perfectly well without metaphor. We have found, on the contrary, that metaphor is pervasive in everyday life, not just in language but in thought and action. Our ordinary conceptual system, in terms of which we both think and act, is fundamentally metaphorical in nature.

2 The concepts that govern our thought are not just matters of the intellect. They also govern our everyday functioning, down to the most mundane details. Our concepts structure what we perceive, how we get around in the world, and how we relate to other people. Our conceptual system thus plays a central role in defining our everyday realities. If we are right in suggesting that our conceptual system is largely metaphorical, then the way we think, what we experience, and what we do every day is very much a matter of metaphor.

出典：Lakoff, George & Mark Johnson. 1980. *Metaphors We Live by*. Chicago: University of Chicago Press. pp. 3–6.（邦訳：渡部昇一・楠瀬淳三・下谷和幸訳『レトリックと人生』大修館書店）メタファーが人間の思考の根源にあることを示し、言葉の観察から人間の世界観に迫った書籍。1980年代以降盛んとなる認知言語学のさきがけとなった。

[5] **get along**　「うまくやっていける」
[7] **in terms of which we both think and act**　= we both think and act in terms of our ordinary conceptual system (and that system is fundamentally metaphorical in nature)
[10] **down to the most mundane details**　「日常の細部に至るまで」
[11] **structure**　「形作る」
[11] **get around in the world**　「世界で生きていく」

3 But our conceptual system is not something we are normally aware of. In most of the little things we do every day, we simply think and act more or less automatically along certain lines. Just what these lines are is by no means obvious. One way to find out is by looking at language. Since communication is based on the same conceptual system that we use in thinking and acting, language is an important source of evidence for what that system is like.

4 Primarily on the basis of linguistic evidence, we have found that most of our ordinary conceptual system is metaphorical in nature. And we have found a way to begin to identify in detail just what the metaphors are that structure how we perceive, how we think, and what we do.

5 To give some idea of what it could mean for a concept to be metaphorical and for such a concept to structure an everyday activity, let us start with the concept ARGUMENT and the conceptual metaphor ARGUMENT IS WAR. This metaphor is reflected in our everyday language by a wide variety of expressions:

ARGUMENT IS WAR
Your claims are *indefensible*.
He *attacked every weak point* in my argument.
His criticisms were *right on target*.
I *demolished* his argument.
I've never *won* an argument with him.
You disagree? Okay, *shoot*!
If you use that *strategy*, he'll *wipe you out*.
He *shot down* all of my arguments.

6 It is important to see that we don't just *talk* about arguments in terms of war. We can actually win or lose arguments. We see the person we are arguing with as an opponent. We attack his positions and we defend our own. We gain and lose ground. We plan and use strategies. If we find a position indefensible, we can abandon it and take a new line of attack. Many of the things we *do* in arguing are partially structured by the concept of war. Though there is no physical

---

[3] **along certain lines** 「一定の手順に沿って」
[21] **shoot** 「言ってみな」発話を促す口語的な表現。
[22] **wipe out** 「全滅させる」転じて議論で負かすということ。
[23] **shoot down** 「撃ち落とす」
[26] **gain and lose ground** 「陣地を獲得したり失ったりする」転じて「優勢になる（gain ground）」、「劣勢になる（lose ground）」。このように慣用的な意味拡張もメタファー的なプロセスに基づいている。
[28] **a new line of attack** 「新しい攻撃路線」

battle, there is a verbal battle, and the structure of an argument—attack, defense, counterattack, etc.—reflects this. It is in this sense that the ARGUMENT IS WAR metaphor is one that we live by in this culture; it structures the actions we perform in arguing.

7　Try to imagine a culture where arguments are not viewed in terms of war, where no one wins or loses, where there is no sense of attacking or defending, gaining or losing ground. Imagine a culture where an argument is viewed as a dance, the participants are seen as performers, and the goal is to perform in a balanced and aesthetically pleasing way. In such a culture, people would view arguments differently, experience them differently, carry them out differently, and talk about them differently. But *we* would probably not view them as arguing at all: they would simply be doing something different. It would seem strange even to call what they were doing "arguing." Perhaps the most neutral way of describing this difference between their culture and ours would be to say that we have a discourse form structured in terms of battle and they have one structured in terms of dance.

8　This is an example of what it means for a metaphorical concept, namely, ARGUMENT IS WAR, to structure (at least in part) what we do and how we understand what we are doing when we argue. *The essence of metaphor is understanding and experiencing one kind of thing in terms of another.* It is not that arguments are a subspecies of war. Arguments and wars are different kinds of things—verbal discourse and armed conflict—and the actions performed are different kinds of actions. But ARGUMENT is partially structured, understood, performed, and talked about in terms of WAR. The concept is metaphorically structured, the activity is metaphorically structured, and, consequently, the language is metaphorically structured.

9　Moreover, this is the *ordinary* way of having an argument and talking about one. The normal way for us to talk about attacking a position is to use the words "attack a position." Our conventional ways of talking about arguments presuppose a metaphor we are hardly ever conscious of. The metaphor is not merely in the words we use—it is in our very concept of an argument. The language of

[1]　**verbal**　「口頭の」
[3]　**live by ...**　「…に頼って生きる」
[9]　**aesthetically pleasing way**　「美学的に見て美しい方法」
[14]　**discourse form**　「対話形式」
[16]　what it means for ~ to do ... の構文に注意。「~が…することが意味するところ」の意味。
[28]　**presuppose**　「前提とする」
[30]　**The language ... it is literal.**　ごく自然に浸透しているため、議論について使われる言葉は詩的なことではなくそのまま文字通りであると感じられるということ。

argument is not poetic, fanciful, or rhetorical; it is literal. We talk about arguments that way because we conceive of them that way—and we act according to the way we conceive of things.

10. The most important claim we have made so far is that metaphor is not just a matter of language, that is, of mere words. We shall argue that, on the contrary, human *thought processes* are largely metaphorical. This is what we mean when we say that the human conceptual system is metaphorically structured and defined. Metaphors as linguistic expressions are possible precisely because there are metaphors in a person's conceptual system. *(1006 words)* [5]

• Language and Thought •

◆ Pre-class Task

Read the passage above. Mark each sentence as T (True) or F (False).

☞ 1

1. Metaphors are merely rhetorical flourishes used in a poetic context. (   )

☞ 2

2. Our everyday realities are mainly defined by our conceptual system. (   )

☞ 3

3. Our conceptual system is more or less automatic and hard to be noticed. (   )

☞ 5

4. *Defeat someone in argument* can be considered as part of the ARGUMENT IS WAR metaphor. (   )

☞ 6

5. "Argument" and "war" share a similar structure. (   )

☞ 7

6. The form of argument is approximately the same when it is viewed as dance and viewed as war. (   )

☞ 8

7. ARGUMENT is a subcategory of WAR. (   )

☞ 9

8. When we talk about arguments, we unconsciously use expressions derived from a metaphor. (   )

65

◆ In-class Task

Warm-up

What metaphor do you think is behind the following sentences? Share your ideas with your group.

1.

I <u>spent</u> one hour cleaning the window.

In technology based industries <u>the time costs</u> of training new employees is high.

Templates will <u>save</u> you a lot of time to write a business email.

We can't give up because we have <u>invested</u> many years in this project.

| TIME IS _____ . |

2.

The sales of our company are on course for recovery.

We need a fresh viewpoint; otherwise our company will be on the rocks.

This is not just the problem of the accounting section—we are in the same boat.

The manager decided to run a tight ship on the budget for research and development.

| _____ IS _____ . |

Reading Comprehension

☞ 3

1. How can we be aware of our conceptual system? Extract a sentence that best describes the method.

_____

☞ 5-6

2. What are the similarities and differences between an actual war and argument as a war?

Similarities

_____
_____
_____
_____
_____

Differences
_____

☞ 9

3. Why is it difficult for us to be aware of metaphors?
_____
_____

☞ 10

4. What is the main claim of the authors? Summarize the final paragraph in your own words.
_____
_____

LISTENING: Examples of Metaphor

 ▶ 12

What are the messages in these images? How can you explain the message? Write a sentence for each image below.

1.   2.

  1. Love is _____
  2. Life is _____

Discuss with your partner why you wrote this idea, and think of one or two examples to support this idea.

67

• LESSON 6 •

 Word Focus

What words or expressions can you think of that are important to understanding metaphors? Write **6 words** you learned from your research and their **definition**.

concept (n.)	an idea of what something is and how it works

Listening 1: Short Summary

Listen to the passage and complete this summary of the listening using the following words in their correct forms (use 4 of the 5 words).

> understand (v.)   explain (v.)   conceptual (adj.)   practice (v.)   connect (v.)

When we use a _____ metaphor, it helps us to _____ our ideas clearly and completely; this type of metaphor directly _____ the event or activity with a feeling that everyone can _____.

Listening 2: Question & Answer

Listen again to the passage and answer the following questions. You can use the box below to write notes.

1. According to the speaker, why do we use metaphors without thinking?

2. The speaker talks about "jobs" as a common thing that metaphors are connected to. What are three other common things he mentions?

3. What does the speaker say is the difference between "a real cost" and "a mistake is a cost"?

68

• Language and Thought •

4. Why does the speaker say that "this past week was hell" is a useful metaphor?

   _____
   _____

5. Why does the speaker say we have to be careful about using metaphors in other languages?

   _____
   _____

Notes

True / False

Using your notes, discuss with your partner whether the following statements are true or false. Circle the correct answer and explain your decision.

1.	The speaker talks about three types of metaphor.	True False
2.	The speaker explains that metaphors are not common, so we should be careful about using them.	True False
3.	The speaker explains the metaphor "a mistake is a cost" by using the example of family life.	True False
4.	According to the speaker, it is difficult to use metaphors from other languages.	True False
5.	The speaker asks the students to practice explaining metaphors to each other.	True False

DISCUSSION

Can you think of any English expressions that are thought to be based on the MIND IS A CONTAINER metaphor? The following words may be helpful: **open, close, fill with, mind, heart, soul.**

A STEP FORWARD

Look up the following word and write a definition with some examples.
　　metonymy

_____

_____

FURTHER READING

[1] 瀬戸賢一（2005）。『よくわかる比喩―ことばの根っこをもっと知ろう』研究社。
[2] 谷口一美（2003）。『認知意味論の新展開―メタファーとメトニミー』（英語学モノグラフシリーズ20）研究社。
[3] 辻幸夫編（2013）。『新編　認知言語学キーワード事典』研究社。
[4] Kövecses, Zoltán (2005). *Metaphor in Culture: Universality and Variation.* Cambridge: Cambridge University Press.

[1]は一般向けにメタファーについて書かれた書籍で、日本語を中心に豊富な例が提示されており、この分野の入門書として最適である。[2]もよい入門書であるが、内容はより学術的なものとなっている。本章で登場した概念メタファーだけではなく、メタファーをよりベーシックなレベルに還元して考えるプライマリーメタファーについても紹介されている。[3]は、メタファーを分析する際に足場となる認知言語学の用語をまとめたものである。本格的に勉強を始めたい人は是非手元に置いておきたい。[4]は、メタファーの普遍性と文化差を論じた書籍である。平易な英語で書かれており、英語・日本語以外のメタファーの例も豊富に含まれている。

LESSON 7 Silent Spring

INTRODUCTION

　レイチェル・カーソンの『沈黙の春』は、環境問題を世界中の人々に広く認識させ、国連人間環境会議やアース・デイなどの現代の環境運動立ち上げのきっかけとなった、20世紀に書かれた最も影響力の大きい書物の一つです。アメリカ合衆国では、本書を読んだジョン・F・ケネディ大統領（当時）が環境問題に強い関心を示し、農薬に関する調査を進めました。その結果、1969年に国家環境政策法が制定され、1970年には国民の健康維持と自然環境の保護を目的として環境保護庁（EPA）が設立されました。さらに、本書の影響はアメリカ合衆国内にとどまらず、初めての環境に関する国際会議となる1972年の国連人間環境会議の開催につながりました。以下の年表で、現在までに日本国内外でどのような環境問題が起こり、どのような取り組みが行われてきたかを簡単に振り返ってみましょう。

1891	足尾銅山鉱毒事件について田中正造が国会で追及する。
1945	広島・長崎原爆投下。
1952	ビキニ環礁でアメリカが水爆実験に成功（旧ソ連は翌年成功）。第五福竜丸が被ばく。
1956	水俣病患者が公式確認される。
1960	ベトナム戦争（–75年）で枯葉剤が使用される。
1962	レイチェル・カーソンが『沈黙の春』を発表する。
1968	富山イタイイタイ病公害訴訟。カネミ油症事件。
1972	国連人間環境会議（ストックホルム）。「人間環境宣言」採択。
1975	土呂久ヒ素公害訴訟。六価クロム汚染事件。
1979	長距離越境大気汚染条約締結（ジュネーブ・酸性雨対策）。スリーマイル島原発事故（アメリカ）。
1986	チェルノブイリ原発事故（旧ソ連）。
1988	オゾン保護法制定（国際）。尼崎大気汚染公害訴訟。
1990	豊島産廃問題が明らかになる。
1999	東海村JCO臨界事故。ダイオキシン類対策特別法制定。
2001	残留性有機汚染物質に関するストックホルム条約採択（多国間条約）。
2008	生物多様性基本法制定。
2011	東京電力福島第一原発事故。

AIM & OBJECTIVE

CONTENT

　1962年に出版されたこの書物でレイチェル・カーソンは、巨大な力を獲得した人類が、地球環境に対して多大な影響を与えていると述べています。人類がどのようにして環境を汚染していたと述べられているかを理解しましょう。

● LESSON 7 ●

> **LANGUAGE**
>
> このレッスンの英文では、筆者は自分の主張を効果的に伝えるためにメタファーを数多く用いています。メタファーがどのように用いられているかを理解していきましょう。また、リスニングではこのレッスンのトピックに関する講義を聞き、内容理解や要約などの訓練を行います。

READING: The Obligation to Endure

◆ Key Words & Phrases

contaminate / pollute	contaminate は、（廃棄物・放射性物質・病原菌・異物などで）汚染する、不潔（不純）な物との接触によって不潔（不純）にする、の意味。pollute は、（水・空気・土地などを）危険なまでに汚染する、（特に廃棄物などで環境を）汚染する、の意味。
strontium 90	ストロンチウム90。ストロンチウムの放射性同位元素の一つで、人体に有害である。radio strontium ともいう。
fallout	（空からの）降下物。（特に核爆発からの）放射性降下物、放射能灰。
insecticide	殺虫剤、防虫剤。
DDT	ディーディーティー（*d*ichloro*d*iphenyl*t*richloroethane の略）。無色・結晶性の防疫用・農業用殺虫剤。自然界で分解されにくいため、長期間にわたり土壌や水循環に残留し、食物連鎖を通じて人間の体内にも取り込まれ、神経毒として作用する。このため、現在日本国内において製造・使用が禁止されているが、一部の発展途上国においてはマラリア予防のために使用されている。

1 The history of life on earth has been a history of interaction between living things and their surroundings. To a large extent, the physical form and the habits of the earth's vegetation and its animal life have been molded by the environment. Considering the whole span of earthly time, the opposite effect, in which life actually modifies its surroundings, has been relatively slight. Only within the moment of time represented by the present century has one species— man—acquired significant power to alter the nature of his world. [5]

出典：Carson, Rachel. 1962. "The Obligations to Endure." *Silent Spring*. London: Penguin. pp. 5–8.
（邦訳：青樹簗一訳『沈黙の春』新潮社）環境問題を世界中の人々に広く認識させ、多くの環境運動立ち上げのきっかけとなった著書。

[5] **Only within ... his world.**　この文は Only within ... century までの副詞句が前置されたために、現在完了形の助動詞 has と 主語 one species—man— が倒置された文となっている。

2. During the past quarter century this power has not only increased to one of disturbing magnitude but it has changed in character. The most alarming of all man's assaults upon the environment is the contamination of air, earth, rivers, and sea with dangerous and even lethal materials. This pollution is for the most part irrecoverable; the chain of evil it initiates not only in the world that must support life but in living tissues is for the most part irreversible. In this now universal contamination of the environment, chemicals are the sinister and little-recognized partners of radiation in changing the very nature of the world—the very nature of its life. (1)<u>Strontium 90, released through nuclear explosions into the air, comes to earth in rain or drifts down as fallout, lodges in soil, enters into the grass or corn or wheat grown there, and in time takes up its abode in the bones of a human being, there to remain until his death.</u> Similarly, chemicals sprayed on croplands or forests or gardens lie long in soil, entering into living organisms, passing from one to another in a chain of poisoning and death. Or they pass mysteriously by underground streams until they emerge and, through the alchemy of air and sunlight, combine into new forms that kill vegetation, sicken cattle, and work unknown harm on those who drink from once pure wells. As Albert Schweitzer has said, "Man can hardly even recognize (2)<u>the devils of his own creation</u>."

3. It took hundreds of millions of years to produce the life that now inhabits the earth—eons of time in which that developing and evolving and diversifying life reached a state of adjustment and balance with its surroundings. The environment, rigorously shaping and directing the life it supported, contained elements that were hostile as well as supporting. Certain rocks gave out dangerous radiation; even within the light of the sun, from which all life draws its energy, there were short-wave radiations with power to injure. Given time—time not in years but in millennia—life adjusts, and a balance has been reached. For time is the essential ingredient; but in the modern world there is no time.

---

[3] **assault**　「(突然の) 襲撃、暴行」ここでは assault が比喩的に用いられ、人類が環境に対して激しい襲撃、攻撃を加えているというようなイメージを出す。このようにアメリカ英語では戦いのイメージをもつ語が比喩的に使われることが多い。以下の flareback, crossfire も同様。
[4] **lethal**　「死をもたらす (力のある)、(毒物・遺伝子など) 致命的な、致死の」
[7] **sinister**　「(差し迫った危険・災いを予示して) 不吉な」
[11] **take up one's abode**　「住居を定める」
[16] **alchemy**　「錬金術」普通の金属を金または銀に変え、また人を不老長寿にする方法を発見しようとした中世の研究。物を変える秘法。
[18] **Albert Schweitzer**　アルザス生まれのドイツ系フランス人の神学者・哲学者・医師・音楽理論家・オルガン演奏家 (1875–1965)。フランス領赤道アフリカ (現在のガボン) での医療奉仕に生涯の多くを捧げた。1952年ノーベル平和賞。
[26] **given time**　「時間が与えられれば」

4. The rapidity of change and the speed with which new situations are created follow the impetuous and heedless pace of man rather than the deliberate pace of nature. Radiation is no longer merely the background radiation of rocks, the bombardment of cosmic rays, the ultraviolet of the sun that have existed before there was any life on earth; radiation is now the unnatural creation of man's tampering with the atom. The chemicals to which life is asked to make its adjustment are no longer merely the calcium and silica and copper and all the rest of the minerals washed out of the rocks and carried in rivers to the sea; they are the synthetic creations of man's inventive mind, brewed in his laboratories, and having no counterparts in nature.

5. To adjust to these chemicals would require time on the scale that is nature's; it would require not merely the years of a man's life but the life of generations. (3)And even this, were it by some miracle possible, would be futile, for the new chemicals come from our laboratories in an endless stream; almost five hundred annually find their way into actual use in the United States alone. The figure is staggering and its implications are not easily grasped—500 new chemicals to which the bodies of men and animals are required somehow to adapt each year, chemicals totally outside the limits of biologic experience.

6. Among them are many that are used in man's war against nature. Since the mid-1940's over 200 basic chemicals have been created for use in killing insects, weeds, rodents, and other organisms described in the modern vernacular as "pests"; and they are sold under several thousand different brand names.

7. These sprays, dusts, and aerosols are now applied almost universally to farms, gardens, forests, and homes—nonselective chemicals that have the power to kill every insect, the "good" and the "bad," to still the song of birds and the leaping of fish in the streams, to coat the leaves with a deadly film, and to linger on in

---

[2] **impetuous**　「性急な、衝動的な」
[3] **background radiation**　「背景放射（線）」岩石などに含まれる自然放射性物質から放出される放射線。
[4] **cosmic ray**　「宇宙線」宇宙空間を飛びかっている高エネルギーの粒子。陽子が大部分を占めヘリウムの原子核なども混ざっている。
[4] **the ultraviolet**　=ultraviolet rays
[6] **tamper with**　「みだりに手を入れる、いじくり回す、干渉する」
[9] **synthetic**　「人工的に製造した、合成の、人造の」化学的な処理によって合成され、天然物質の代用となる。
[13] **And even this, were it by some miracle possible, would be futile, ...**　仮定法過去の文。ifを用いて普通の語順にすると以下のようになる：And even this would be futile if it were by some miracle possible, ...
[16] **staggering**　「びっくりするほど大きい、膨大な」
[21] **rodent**　「齧歯動物」ネズミ・リス・ビーバーなど。
[21] **modern vernacular**　「現代風の呼び名」
[22] **pest**　「有害生物、（病）害虫」

soil—all this though the intended target may be only a few weeds or insects. Can anyone believe it is possible to lay down such a barrage of poisons on the surface of the earth without making it unfit for all life? They should not be called "insecticides," but "biocides."

8 The whole process of spraying seems caught up in an endless spiral. Since DDT was released for civilian use, a process of escalation has been going on in which ever more toxic materials must be found. This has happened because insects, in a triumphant vindication of Darwin's principle of the survival of the fittest, have evolved super races immune to the particular insecticide used, hence a deadlier one has always to be developed—and then a deadlier one than that. It has happened also because destructive insects often undergo a "flareback," or resurgence, after spraying, in numbers greater than before. Thus the chemical war is never won, and all life is caught in its violent crossfire.

9 Along with the possibility of the extinction of mankind by nuclear war, the central problem of our age has therefore become the contamination of man's total environment with such substances of incredible potential for harm—substances that accumulate in the tissues of plants and animals and even penetrate the germ cells to shatter or alter the very material of heredity upon which the shape of the future depends. *(1030 words)*

---

[2] **barrage** 「弾幕砲火、弾幕射撃、集中攻撃」農薬などの殺虫剤の使用を、まるで戦争での弾幕砲火のようだと比喩的に表現している。
[8] **in a triumphant vindication of...** 「…を勝ち誇ったように立証して」
[11] **flareback** 「後炎」発砲後の砲尾や溶鉱炉などから出る火災の逆流。ここでは比喩的に「激しい反撃」。
[13] **crossfire** 「十字火、十字砲火、交差射撃」2点以上の地点から一つの対象をねらって交差的に浴びせる砲火。

● LESSON 7 ●

◆ Pre-class Task
Read the passage above. Mark each sentence as T (True) or F (False).

☞ 1
1. Since the beginning of the 20th Century man has developed a significant ability to alter the very nature of the planet. (   )

☞ 2
2. Most of the contamination caused by dangerous chemicals can be removed. (   )
3. Chemicals can pass through the groundwater and do harm to plants and animals. (   )

☞ 3
4. Nature can sometimes be hostile to plants and animals. (   )

☞ 4
5. Background radiation existed long before there was any life on the earth. (   )

☞ 7
6. Sprays and aerosols have the power to kill only "bad" insects. (   )

☞ 8
7. Since DDT was released for civilian use, efforts have been made to develop more poisonous chemicals. (   )

☞ 9
8. The only problem of our age is the contamination of the environment with harmful chemicals. (   )

• Silent Spring •

◆ In-class Task

Work in pairs. Human beings have accomplished a lot of advances at the expense of the environment. What kind of pollution is the most alarming to the environment? From the list below, choose the most serious environmental pollution. Give reasons and an explanation for your choice.

    A) atmospheric pollution
    B) agrochemical pollution
    C) radioactive pollution
    D) marine pollution

☞ 2

1. Read the underlined part (1). What kind of metaphor is used to explain the effects of strontium 90? Choose one of the three choices below and give a reason for your choice.
    A) Strontium 90 is a creature.
    B) Strontium 90 is a war.
    C) Strontium 90 is a medicine.

    _____
    _____
    _____

2. Explain the underlined part (2), "the devils of his own creation," with the two examples given in the paragraph 2.

    _____
    _____
    _____

☞ 4

3. What kind of change has happened to radiation and chemicals?

    _____
    _____
    _____

• LESSON 7 •

☞ 5

4. Read the underlined sentence (3) and explain why even this would be futile.

___

☞ 7

5. Why should the chemicals be called "biocides" instead of "insecticides?"

___

☞ 8

6. Explain the process of "an endless spiral" with the example of DDT.
   Stage 1: A particular insecticide is used to kill insects.
   Stage 2: _____
   Stage 3: A deadlier insecticide is developed to kill stronger races.
   Stage 4: _____
   The process goes on endlessly. . . .

LISTENING: Rachel Carson *Silent Spring*

Before You Listen

The Finnish cartoonist Seppo Leinonen often creates cartoons to highlight environmental issues.

What point do you think the cartoonist is trying to make in these two cartoons?

78

• Silent Spring •

📖 Word Focus

What words or expressions can you think of that are important to farming and the protection of the environment? Write **6 words** you learned from your research and an **example sentence** using them.

crop (n.)	The main crops were wheat and barley.

🎧 Listening 1: Short Summary

Listen to the passage and complete this summary of the listening using the following words in their correct forms (use 4 of the 5 words).

> masterpiece (n.)   campaign (v.)   environmentalist (adj.)   use (n.)   article (n.)

Rachel Carson, a pioneer of the _____ movement, successfully _____ against the _____ of harmful chemicals in farming in her _____, *Silent Spring*.

● LESSON 7 ●

🎧 Listening 2: Question & Answer

Listen again to the passage and answer the following questions. You can use the box below to write notes.

1. When is World Environment Day?
   _____

2. What is meant by *environmentalism*?
   _____

3. What were the financial benefits of using DDT?
   _____
   _____

4. How did DDT reduce the workload of farmers?
   _____

5. What was the American President's reaction to Rachel Carson's book?
   _____

Notes

🔍 True / False

Using your notes, discuss with your partner whether the following statements are true or false. Circle the correct answer and explain your decision.

1. Carson wrote many books.   True   False

2. DDT kills only harmful insects (i.e. pests).   True   False

3. Larger creatures, such as birds and mice, were unaffected by DDT.   True   False

4. It took Carson a long time to write *Silent Spring*.   True   False

5. President Nixon was influenced by *Silent Spring*.   True   False

DISCUSSION

Since the publication of *Silent Spring* in 1962, we have been making progress in preventing the chemical pollution, but we have still got a long way to go. What kinds of problems remain unsolved, and what must we do to solve the problems? Discuss in groups.

A STEP FORWARD

Search online one of the following modern environmental catastrophes and write a paragraph of about 100 words.

1. The radioactive contamination caused by the accidents at Fukushima First Nuclear Power Plants
2. Minamata Mercury Poisoning

FURTHER READING

[1] 渡邉泉・久野勝治編（2011）。『環境毒性学』朝倉書店。
[2] 常石敬一（2000）。『化学物質は警告する―「悪魔の水」から環境ホルモンまで』洋泉社。

[1] は環境汚染物質と環境毒性について、歴史的背景や実証例をふまえて解説した入門書である。毒性とその発現メカニズムや、生物濃縮などについて詳細に説明されている。[2] は殺虫剤などに含まれる化学物質が引き起こした環境破壊や、それらが内分泌撹乱物質（環境ホルモン）として人体に及ぼす影響などについて分かりやすく書かれた新書である。

LESSON 8 The U.S. Civil Rights Movement

INTRODUCTION

"I Have a Dream" という演説で知られるキング牧師らが率いたアメリカの黒人差別撤廃運動（1950–60年代、いわゆる公民権運動）を象徴する事件があります。1955年アラバマ州モンゴメリーのバス車内で白人に席を譲ることを拒否した黒人女性ローザ・パークスがそれを理由に逮捕されたのです。これまでの不当な人種差別に辟易した人々はバス乗車拒否運動を行い、差別撤廃運動を本格化させました。

アメリカ人種問題の歴史：関連年表

1776　アメリカ独立宣言（Declaration of Independence）。当初、奴隷貿易を非難する文言が含まれる予定であったが、最終的には奴隷制を認める内容となった。

1863　奴隷解放宣言（Emancipation Proclamation）発布。1861年に勃発した南北戦争の終盤、リンカーン大統領が、南部諸州の奴隷解放を宣言。

1909　全米黒人地位向上協会（National Association for the Advancement of Colored People）設立。アメリカで最も歴史のある黒人差別撤廃運動（公民権運動）組織の一つ。略称 NAACP.

1913　ローザ・パークス、アラバマ州に生まれる。

1955　バスで白人乗客に席を譲らなかったため、パークスが逮捕される。モンゴメリー・バス・ボイコット事件に発展。

1963　ワシントン大行進。20万人が人種差別撤廃を求めワシントンDCでデモを行った。キング牧師の有名な "I Have a Dream" 演説はここで行われた。

1964　人種を理由にした差別を禁止する法律「公民権法（Civil Rights Act）」制定。奴隷解放宣言（1863年）になぞらえて「第二の解放宣言（Second Emancipation Proclamation）」と呼ばれるほど、歴史的意義の大きな法律制定となった。

AIM & OBJECTIVE

CONTENT

このレッスンでは、1955年のモンゴメリー・バス乗車拒否運動のきっかけとなったローザ・パークス逮捕事件の経緯を、彼女の回想録を通して学びます。この事件は、アメリカの公民権運動を大きく前進させた出来事として、アメリカの歴史に深く刻まれています。

LANGUAGE

英文の内容を判断するための「根拠」を意識しながら読解を行います。根拠を把握しなが

ら読むことで、英文の内容を論理的に整理した上で理解できるようになります。また、リスニングではこのレッスンのトピックに関する講義を聞き、内容理解や要約などの訓練を行います。

READING: You're Under Arrest

◆ Key Words & Phrases

Civil Rights Movement	アメリカで特に1950–60年代に行われた公民権運動。主に黒人差別撤廃を目指す運動であった。
segregation law	人種隔離を認める法律。奴隷制撤廃後も、アメリカの南部諸州では有色人種、とりわけ黒人の公共施設利用を禁止あるいは制限する法律が多く存在した。これらはまとめてジム・クロウ法（Jim Crow laws）と呼ばれ、1964年に人種差別を禁止する公民権法が制定されるまで効力を発揮していた。
boycott	抗議の意を表明するために商品の不買運動やサービスの利用拒否運動などを行うこと。

1 I don't think any segregation law angered black people in Montgomery more than bus segregation. And that had been so since the laws about segregation on public transportation had been passed. That was back in 1900, and black people had boycotted Montgomery streetcars until the City Council changed its ordinance so that nobody would be forced to give up a seat unless there was another seat to move to. But over the years practices had changed, although the law had not. When I was put off the bus back in 1943, the bus driver was really acting against the law. In 1945, two years after that incident, the State of Alabama passed a law requiring that all bus companies under its jurisdiction enforce segregation. But that law did not spell out what bus drivers were supposed to do in a case like mine.

2 Here it was, half a century after the first segregation law, and there were 50,000

出典：Parks, Rosa & Jim Haskins. 1992. *My Story*. New York: Puffin Books. pp. 108–109, 113–117.（邦訳：高橋朋子訳『ローザ・パークス自伝』潮出版社）「公民権運動の母」と呼ばれたローザ・パークスが若い人々に向けて易しい言葉づかいで綴った自伝。あからさまな黒人差別がはびこる時代に公民権運動の活動家として活躍した彼女の自伝はアメリカ史を知る上で不可欠な1冊と考えられており、今も歴史教育の場などで広く読まれている。

[4] **the City Council**「市議会」
[5] **ordinance**「条例」本文ではlaw（法律）も同じ意味で使われている。
[9] **require**「（法・規則などが）命じる、命令する」
[9] **jurisdiction**「行政管轄区域」ある行政の権力が効力を発揮する地域的範囲を指す。
[10] **enforce**「（法律など）を施行する、（法律として）強要する」

African Americans in Montgomery. More of us rode the buses than Caucasians did, because more whites could afford cars. It was very humiliating having to suffer the indignity of riding segregated buses twice a day, five days a week, to go downtown and work for white people.

★ ★ ★ ★ ★ ★ ★ ★

3. When I got off from work that evening of December 1, I went to Court Square as usual to catch the Cleveland Avenue bus home. I didn't look to see who was driving when I got on, and by the time I recognized him, I had already paid my fare. It was the same driver who had put me off the bus back in 1943, twelve years earlier. He was still tall and heavy, with red, rough-looking skin. And he was still mean-looking. I didn't know if he had been on that route before—they switched the drivers around sometimes. I do know that most of the time if I saw him on a bus, I wouldn't get on it.

4. I saw a vacant seat in the middle section of the bus and took it. I didn't even question why there was a vacant seat even though there were quite a few people standing in the back. If I had thought about it at all, I would probably have figured maybe someone saw me get on and did not take the seat but left it vacant for me. There was a man sitting next to the window and two women across the aisle.

5. The next stop was the Empire Theater, and some whites got on. They filled up the white seats, and one man was left standing. The driver looked back and noticed the man standing. Then he looked back at us. He said, "Let me have those front seats," because they were the front seats of the black section. Didn't anybody move. We just sat right where we were, the four of us. Then he spoke a second time: "Y'all better make it light on yourselves and let me have those seats."

6. The man in the window seat next to me stood up, and I moved to let him pass by me, and then I looked across the aisle and saw that the two women were also standing. I moved over to the window seat. I could not see how standing up was going to "make it light" for me. The more we gave in and complied, the worse

---

[1] **Caucasian** 「白色人種」本文では whites も同義語として登場している。
[5] **that evening of December 1** 「1955年12月1日の晩」この日のパークス逮捕がバス・ボイコットのきっかけとなった。
[8] **back in 1943, twelve years earlier** 「12年前の1943年」パークスは1943年にも人種差別的な慣例に従わなかったためバスを降ろされるという経験をしている。
[22] **Didn't anybody move.** 「誰も席を立たなかった」Nobody moved. の口語表現。本書はパークスの語りを綴った自伝であるため、多くの南部的口語表現がそのまま記録されている。
[24] **Y'all** 「みんな、お前たち」You all を意味する南部的口語表現。

they treated us.

7. I thought back to the time when I used to sit up all night and didn't sleep, and my grandfather would have his gun right by the fireplace, or if he had his one-horse wagon going anywhere, he always had his gun in the back of the wagon. People always say that I didn't give up my seat because I was tired, but that isn't true. I was not tired physically, or no more tired than I usually was at the end of a working day. I was not old, although some people have an image of me as being old then. I was forty-two. No, the only tired I was, was tired of giving in.

8. The driver of the bus saw me still sitting there, and he asked was I going to stand up. I said, "No." He said, "Well, I'm going to have you arrested." Then I said, "You may do that." These were the only words we said to each other. I didn't even know his name, which was James Blake, until we were in court together. He got out of the bus and stayed outside for a few minutes, waiting for the police.

9. As I sat there, I tried not to think about what might happen. I knew that anything was possible. I could be manhandled or beaten. I could be arrested. People have asked me if it occurred to me then that I could be the test case the NAACP had been looking for. I did not think about that at all. In fact if I had let myself think too deeply about what might happen to me, I might have gotten off the bus. But I chose to remain.

10. Meanwhile there were people getting off the bus and asking for transfers, so that began to loosen up the crowd, especially in the back of the bus. Not everyone got off, but everybody was very quiet. What conversation there was, was in low tones; no one was talking out loud. It would have been quite interesting to have seen the whole bus empty out. Or if the other three had stayed where they were, because if they'd had to arrest four of us instead of one, then that would have given me a little support. But it didn't matter. I never thought hard of them at all and never even bothered to criticize them.

11. Eventually two policemen came. They got on the bus, and one of them asked me why I didn't stand up. I asked him, "Why do you all push us around?" He said to me, and I quote him exactly, "I don't know, but the law is the law and you're under arrest." *(1019 words)*

---

[3] **my grandfather**　祖父は彼女に「ひどい扱いに屈してはいけない」ということを教えた人物であった。
[16] **manhandle**　「手荒く扱う、襲う」
[17] **People have asked ... looking for.**　当時 NAACP はバスの人種隔離をめぐってモンゴメリー市当局を告訴することを考えており、そのためには明確な訴訟事実となる事例が必要だと考えられていた。パークスが運転手の命令に背いたのは、自らがその事例となるための政治的判断だったのではないかと疑われてきた、とパークスは述べている。

• LESSON 8 •

◆ Pre-class Task

Read the passage above. Mark each sentence as T (True) or F (False).

☞ 1

1. In 1900, black people in Montgomery had a streetcar boycott, but the City Council kept its segregation law legal. (   )
2. Back then, bus drivers were not well-informed how to react to complicated situations such as this incident. (   )

☞ 2

3. Lower wages and incomes resulted in higher rates of black passengers on buses and public transportations. (   )

☞ 3

4. On December 1, 1955, Parks decided not to get on a bus to go home because she knew the driver and did not like him. (   )

☞ 4

5. Among the figures below, A) shows the bus seat Parks first took on that day. (   )

☞ 5

6. The black passengers except Parks immediately gave their seats to white passengers. (   )

☞ 6

7. In paragraph 6 "make it light" means "punish." (   )

☞ 7

8. Parks would not give up her seat for white people because she felt tired after work. (   )

☞ 8 - 9

9. The driver arrested Parks right after her protest. (   )

☞ 10 - 11

10. The mood of the bus was peaceful and quiet. (   )

◆ In-class Task

Warm-up

Name a historical figure who has fought against discrimination. What did s/he accomplish?

Reading Comprehension

☞ 3

1. What impression did Parks have of the bus driver? Explain why you think so by quoting some phrases she used to describe him.
   I think she had _____
   because she used words like _____

☞ 6

2. Which of the following is the closest in meaning to "the worse they treated us?"
   A) They would behave toward us more roughly.
   B) They would humiliate us more secretly.
   C) They would hurt us less obviously.
   D) They would insult us less passionately.

☞ 7

3. A) Find the sentence in which Parks explains the fundamental reason why she had refused to give up her seat. B) Why did you think it is the fundamental reason?
   A) _____
   B) _____
   _____

• LESSON 8 •

☞ 8 - 9

4. Why did Parks try not to think "what might happen?" Explain it by quoting some phrases from the text.

_____
_____

LISTENING: The Second Emancipation Proclamation

 ▶ 16

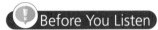

Here are some hints connected to three important events concerning the American Civil Rights Movement. Can you guess what the events are and who the famous people are?

April 15, 1947	December 1, 1955	August 28, 1963
Dodgers (42)	Bus boycott	200,000 people
J. R.	R. P.	M. L. K.
New York	Alabama	Tennessee

What is it? _____   What is it? _____   What is it? _____
Who is it? _____   Who is it? _____   Who is it? _____

Word Focus

What words or expressions can you think of that are important to understanding the Civil Rights Movement? Write **3 words** you learned from your research and their **definition**.

riot (n.)	noisy, violent and uncontrolled behavior by a large group
inferior (adj.)	lower in status; second class

• The U.S. Civil Rights Movement •

Listening 1: Short Summary

Listen to the passage and complete this summary of the listening using the following words in their correct forms (use 4 of the 5 words).

discrimination (n.)　negative (adj.)　positive (adj.)　prejudice (n.)　damage (n.)

The Civil Rights Movement saw many atrocious acts stemming from racial _____. These acts of _____ had extremely _____ psychological effects on black children who were labeled 'inferior.' However, thanks to the many voices of protest, _____ changes were made.

Listening 2: Question & Answer

Listen again to the passage and answer the following questions. You can use the box below to write notes.

1. What are the two things the speaker clarifies in this lecture?
   _____

2. What happened after Parks's arrest to cause the law to change?
   _____

3. According to the speaker, what is the difference between "prejudice" and "discrimination?"
   _____

4. Why does the speaker say that victims of discrimination are damaged psychologically?
   _____

5. What ruling did the U.S. Supreme Court unanimously agree upon?
   _____

Notes　Tip: When two terms are being talked about, a column note format is useful.

• LESSON 8 •

 **True / False**

Using your notes, discuss with your partner whether the following statements are true or false. Circle the correct answer and explain your decision.

1. 1955 was a significant year in the Civil Rights Movement, as immediately following the arrest of Parks, blacks could take any seat on a bus.   True   False

2. According to the speaker, prejudice is a part of our everyday life as we all tend to make inferences without knowing all the facts.   True   False

3. Rosa Parks's arrest, according to the speaker, is an example of prejudice.   True   False

4. Chief Justice Earl Warren was one of the main voices of protest that fought against segregation in schools.   True   False

5. The most important voice of protest in the stand against segregation was the President of the United States.   True   False

DISCUSSION

What discrimination have you faced or witnessed firsthand in your life? How did you react to it? Discrimination sometimes happens when people from different national or ethnic groups don't know each other well. Discuss how your university or organization tries to increase intercultural understanding. Suggest methods they could use to increase this kind of understanding.

A STEP FORWARD

Look up the terms shown below and write what it means in your own words.

political correctness

_____

_____

affirmative action

_____

_____

FURTHER READING

［1］上岡伸雄編（2006）。『名演説で学ぶアメリカの歴史』研究社。
［2］ノーサップ、ソロモン（2014）。『12イヤーズ ア スレーブ』小岩雅美訳、花泉社。
［3］本田創造（1991）。『アメリカ黒人の歴史』岩波書店。
［4］上杉忍（2013）。『アメリカ黒人の歴史―奴隷貿易からオバマ大統領まで』中央公論新社。

［1］はアメリカ史において重要な役割を果たした多くの名演説を英語で収録したもの。キング牧師の"I Have a Dream"演説も収録されている。全編対訳および朗読CDもついており、アメリカ史の概略を学びながら英語力を磨くことができる。［2］は19世紀のアメリカ北部で、奴隷ではない自由黒人として生まれ育ったソロモン・ノーサップの自伝の日本語翻訳版。原題は *Twelve Years a Slave*（1853）。ある日突然誘拐され、12年の歳月を奴隷として生き延びたノーサップのこの書は2013年に映画化され、話題となった（映画邦題『それでも夜は明ける』）。［3］［4］は、アメリカ独立前後から現代までのアメリカ黒人史の重要な事件・出来事の数々が社会的分析とともに解説されている。タイトル通りアメリカ黒人の歴史を一通り学ぶ上で最適の2冊。［4］はアメリカ初の黒人大統領オバマに関する分析もカバーしている。

LESSON 9 Human Genes

INTRODUCTION

　2000年初頭に完了したヒトゲノム解読から15年ほどが経過し、一般社会にも「ゲノム」や「遺伝子」等の科学用語が浸透してきました。遺伝子の正体はDNAという化学物質であり、A（アデニン）、T（チミン）、C（シトシン）、G（グアニン）というたった4つの塩基が多数整列し、3つ並びの塩基からアミノ酸が決定し、それがタンパク質を構成します。これは、遺伝子が「情報」であり、遺伝情報が酵素（タンパク質）という「機能」へとつながることを意味します。ヒトの遺伝子配列は人種を問わずほとんど同じ（99.9％以上は同じ）ですが、わずか0.1％は異なることが知られています。この0.1％の差異の中には個

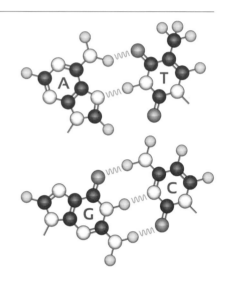

人を特徴づける形質（身長や性格等）が含まれていますが、その割合は0.1％よりも少ないと今日では理解されています。これら遺伝学への一般的な理解は進んできましたが、未だに遺伝子についての誤解は残っており、遺伝子全体の機能を解明する研究が進んでいます。

AIM & OBJECTIVE

CONTENT

　遺伝子の働きについて一般的な見方が紹介されます。遺伝子がどのような構造であるのか、そして遺伝子が私たち一人ひとり、あるいは人類と他の生物との違いをどのようにもたらしているのか、遺伝子の働きに関する私たちの誤解とは何なのかを考えていきます。

LANGUAGE

　英文に書かれていることから著者が本当に言いたいことを理解する読解練習を行います。英文の内容をヒントにして、推論を用いながら著者の真意を読み解いてみましょう。また、リスニングではこのレッスンのトピックに関する講義を聞き、内容理解や要約などの訓練を行います。

READING: What Are Genes for?

◆ Key Words & Phrases

gene	遺伝子。遺伝情報の単位で、染色体上の決まった位置に座上し、各遺伝子が発現すると伝令 RNA（mRNA）を介してタンパク質合成が行われる。
deoxyribonucleic acid（DNA）	デオキシリボ核酸。塩基、五単糖（デオキシリボース）、リン酸からなるヌクレオチドが重合した高分子で、二重らせん構造をとる。
base	塩基。塩基には A（アデニン）、T（チミン）、C（シトシン）、G（グアニン）があり、A と T、C と G は相補的な関係にあり、それぞれ二重および三重の水素結合をなす。この結合によってDNA が安定な状態を保っている。
enzyme	酵素。生体で起こる化学反応に対して触媒として機能する分子。
dopamine	ドーパミン。中枢神経系に存在する神経伝達物質で、運動調節、ホルモン調節、快の感情、意欲や学習等に関わる。
chromosome	染色体。ヒストンと呼ばれるタンパク質に DNA が巻きついた棒状の固まりで、ヒトの場合一つの細胞の中に22対の常染色体と1対の性染色体が現れる。

1 Alexandra was naturally shy largely because of her genes, but genes are not switches that say "shy" or "outgoing," or "happy" or "sad." Genes are simply chemicals that direct the combination of more chemicals. The chemical that makes up genes is called deoxyribonucleic acid, or DNA. It comprises simple building blocks called bases, of which there are just four different varieties: A, G, [5] C, and T. The bases come together in long strings, and each DNA molecule consists of two of these strings paired according to the rule that A matches T and G matches C. DNA stores information in the order of bases. The DNA sequence "AGCT" means one thing, and the sequence "TCGA" something else, as different in meaning as "taps" and "spat." [10]

2 The information in DNA is converted into proteins, which are made of amino

---

出典：Hamer, Dean & Peter Copeland. 1998. *Living with Our Genes.* New York: Doubleday. pp. 17–20.（邦訳：吉田利子訳『遺伝子があなたをそうさせる―喫煙からダイエットまで』草思社）著者の一人であるヘイマーは、遺伝子と性的指向に関する研究を1993年に発表し、話題となった。本書には、遺伝子と行動の関係が平易に書かれており、近年の行動遺伝学研究の動向を一般に広めるきっかけとなった。

[2] **outgoing**「外向的」
[4] **comprise**「…からなる」
[6] **molecule**「分子」物質に固有な性質をそなえた最小の粒子。
[11] **protein**「タンパク質」。20種のアミノ酸がジスルフィド結合（アミド結合）により結合した高次構造を有する分子を指す。
[11] **amino acid**「アミノ酸」

acids. Proteins are where the action is. The most important function of proteins is to act as enzymes that change one chemical into another. For example, it's an enzyme that converts tyrosine, an amino acid found in many foods, into dopamine, a brain chemical that can make you feel active and excited. A different enzyme breaks down the dopamine into smaller molecules and thereby leaves you feeling more relaxed or even lazy. Different enzymes make and degrade the more than 300 brain chemicals that influence thinking, acting, and feeling.

[3] The brain and body are built by DNA, and everyone's DNA is pretty much the same. We all have 99.9 percent the same DNA as Michael Jordan, Albert Einstein, Elizabeth Taylor, Charles Manson, Julius Caesar, Julia Child, and Jules Verne. All of them and everyone who has ever lived have the same 100,000 or so genes, which are organized into the same 23 chromosomes.

[4] But "pretty much the same" is not exactly the same. There are differences in DNA—about 0.1 percent, or 1 bit out of every 1,000. Considering that there are 3 billion chemical bases in question, the differences matter. Where Michael Jordan's DNA says "G," Michael Jackson's may say "C," and Andrew Jackson's said "T," while Jack the Ripper's said "A." There are roughly 3 million such differences between individuals, and these differences are responsible for all the inherited aspects of the variations among people, from eye color to height to personality or intelligence. It's hard to believe that such a tiny difference—one-tenth of 1 percent—could make such a great difference in how people turn out, yet this percentage is actually an exaggeration. Many of the 3 million variations

---

[3] **tyrosine** 「チロシン」アドレナリン・チロキシン・メラニン色素を形成するもとになるアミノ酸。
[3] **convert tyrosine into dopamine** という構文に注意。tyrosine, dopamine を説明するためにそれぞれコンマの後に同格名詞句が用いられている。
[5] **thereby** 「それによって」
[7] **degrade** 「分解する」
[10] **Michael Jordan** バスケットボールの神様と評されるアメリカの元バスケットボール選手 (1963–)。
[10] **Albert Einstein** ドイツ生まれのユダヤ人理論物理学者 (1879–1955)。
[11] **Elizabeth Taylor** ハリウッド黄金時代を代表するイギリス出身の女優 (1932–2011)。
[11] **Charles Manson** 1960年代末から1970年代初め頃のアメリカのカルト指導者で犯罪者 (1934–)。
[11] **Julius Caesar** 共和制ローマ期の政治家 (100–44 B.C.)。
[11] **Julia Child** 1960年代に「アメリカの料理の母」と呼ばれた料理研究家 (1912–2004)。
[11] **Jules Verne** サイエンス・フィクションの開祖として19世紀後半に活躍したフランスの小説家 (1828–1905)。
[16] **matter** (v.)「問題となる」
[17] **Michael Jackson** キング・オブ・ポップと称されるアメリカのエンターテイナー (1958–2009)。
[17] **Andrew Jackson** アメリカの軍人・政治家・黒人奴隷農場主で第7代アメリカ合衆国大統領 (1767–1845)。
[18] **Jack the Ripper** 「切り裂きジャック」1888年にイギリスで連続発生した猟奇殺人事件の犯人の通称。
[19] **be responsible for ...** 「…の主要因である」

don't mean anything as far as we know, so there are even fewer differences that matter.

5. If you still don't believe that 0.1 percent of DNA could be responsible for so many differences, consider the fact that human DNA differs from chimpanzee DNA by only 1 to 2 percent; your DNA and a chimp's are at least 98 percent the same. Yet this seemingly "fine print" of DNA instructions is the reason humans can do calculus, compose poetry, and build cathedrals, while chimps pick bugs off each other and eat them. Humans have pretty much the same DNA as a chimp because that's where we came from; and the chimp is close to the ape because that's where he came from; and so on down the line to fish and reptiles and even single-cell organisms such as yeast. This evolutionary conservation has a beneficial side effect: we can often figure out what a human gene does by looking at a similar gene in simpler organisms.

6. One of the most common misconceptions about genetics is that there are genes "for" things. Some people have the genes "for" breast cancer, shyness, blue eyes, and so they must have the disease, condition, or trait. This is what people tend to think when they hear about a gene "for" depression, or a "gay gene," or "obesity gene." If that were true, it would be easy enough to undergo testing to see what genes you have, and therefore what you ought to worry about. That's not the way it works. Everyone has a "mood gene," and a "sexual orientation gene," and a gene that regulates body weight. The difference is that the genes come in different varieties or flavors.

7. For example, maybe the "mood gene," which everyone has, makes a receptor protein that responds to the hormones released under stress. Maybe the only difference between two people is that one has a gene with T at position 4,356, whereas the other person has a C at the same spot. That might be enough to affect the strength of the electrical current flowing through the cells, so the same amount of hormone produces a gentle buzz in one person and a walloping jolt

---

[5] chimp （口語）= chimpanzee
[6] fine print 「細目」契約書などで小さい字で書かれた部分のことで、DNAのわずかな違いが与える指令のことを喩えている。
[7] do calculus 「微積分をする」
[8] bug 「小さい虫」
[10] down the line 「(過程の) ある時点で」
[11] reptile 「爬虫類」
[11] yeast 「イースト、酵母」
[14] misconception 「誤った考え」
[28] buzz 「(気持ちの) ざわめき」
[28] walloping jolt 「(精神的に) 大きな衝撃」

in another. That single detail—1 letter out of 3 billion—could mean the difference between a mostly cheerful person and one who is easily depressed. Both people have the same gene, but the fine print makes all the difference. Imagine a room filled with 30,000 books. Here the difference would be the equivalent of a single letter in a single book. *(850 words)* [5]

• Human Genes •

◆ Pre-class Task
Read the passage above. Mark each sentence as T (True) or F (False).

☞ 1
1. Genes are the only chemicals that determine the personality such as "shy" or "outgoing" or "happy" or "sad." (   )

☞ 2
2. The only function of enzymes is to change one chemical into another. (   )

☞ 3 - 4
3. Because DNA has 3 billion chemical bases, even 0.1 percent difference of DNA between individuals is noticeable. (   )

☞ 5
4. A one to two percent difference of DNA between humans and chimps does not matter. (   )

☞ 6
5. Some people have the genes for breast cancer or blue eyes, while others have the genes for depression or obesity. (   )

☞ 7
6. Although people have the same gene that controls mood, a small change in this gene can have a large effect on the person's feelings and personality. (   )

• LESSON 9 •

◆ In-class Task

Try to draw images of DNA and chromosomes. Compare each drawing with your partner.

DNA	Chromosomes

Reading Comprehension

☞ 1

1. Choose the sentence that DOES NOT fit the content of this paragraph.
   A) Alexandra was naturally shy because she does not have an "outgoing" gene.
   B) There are only two pairing patterns in DNA bases: A-T and G-C.
   C) "DNA" stands for "deoxyribonucleic acid."
   D) Two DNA sequences "AGCT" and "TCGA" are different in meaning.

☞ 2

2. Complete the sentences below by filling in the blanks A)–E) with appropriate words. The same word should be written in the blanks with the same letter.
   ・Tyrosine is an (A) found in many foods, and it can be broken down into brain chemical called (B).
   ・(C)s are made of (A)s based on the information in the (D).
   ・The most important function of (C)s is to act as (E)s that change one chemical into another.
   ・(E)s can break down (B) into smaller molecules.

   A) _____   B) _____   C) _____
   D) _____   E) _____

98

3. What is dopamine made from and what function does it have in our body?
   _____
   _____

☞ 3 - 4

4. There is only 0.1 percent of genetic difference between individuals. Choose the correct sentence that matches with the author's claim regarding this matter.
   A) Though there is only a 1 bit difference out of every 1,000 bases, it is the cause of all the inherited aspects of variation among people.
   B) Though there are roughly 3 million differences between individuals, since many of them are not important (as far as we know), some environmental or cultural factors are connected to the variations among humans.
   C) Though we share almost 99.9 percent of our DNA with each other, 'ordinary' people have fewer sequence differences than 'talented' people such as Michael Jordan and Albert Einstein, so we cannot become like them.
   D) Though it is hard to believe that only one-tenth of 1 percent difference in DNA could make a great difference in how people turn out, it is a convincing fact because all 3 million differences have very important effects.

5. Why do you think the author uses Michael Jordan, Michael Jackson, Andrew Jackson and Jack the Ripper as examples in this paragraph?
   _____
   _____

☞ 5

6. Explain why the author refers to 1 to 2 percent difference of DNA between humans and chimps.
   _____
   _____
   _____

☞ 6

7. What is a misconception regarding a "gay gene?"
   _____
   _____

• LESSON 9 •

☞ 6 - 7

8. The author states, "<u>The difference is that the genes come in different varieties or flavors.</u>" Explain what the author means in connection to body weight or sexual orientation.

_____
_____

☞ 7

9. Read the "<u>mood gene</u>" example. What kind of neurological difference does the DNA position make in this example?

_____
_____

LISTENING: The *Nature* vs. *Nurture* Debate

Not only your *genes* but also the *environment* you grew up in and *individual choices* throughout life influence who you are. Provide at least one example of how each of these three factors has influenced who you are as a person.

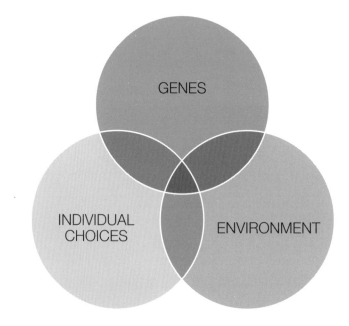

Word Focus

What words or expressions are connected with genes? Write **6 words** you learned from your research and an **example** of how they are connected to your life.

inherit (v.)	My sister inherited the patience of her grandmother.

Listening 1: Short Summary

Listen to the passage and complete this summary of the listening using the following words in their correct forms (use 4 of the 5 words).

nature (n.)   genetic (adj.)   nurture (n.)   environment (n.)   lifestyle (n.)

As individuals, we are influenced by our _____ inheritance, known as _____. However, the _____ in which we grew up can also influence who we are and our success in life. This latter component is known as _____.

• LESSON 9 •

🎧 Listening 2: Question & Answer

Listen again to the passage and answer the following questions. You can use the box below to write notes.

1. How did the speaker try to prevent his hair loss?
   _____

2. Why does the speaker feel sorry for his son?
   _____

3. What mistake did the nurse make at the hospital in Tokyo?
   _____

4. What was different about the boys' education?
   _____

5. Was the compensation from the hospital enough?
   _____

Notes

🔍 True / False

Using your notes, discuss with your partner whether the following statements are true or false. Circle the correct answer and explain your decision.

1.	About 18% of male baldness is hereditary.	True False
2.	"Nurture" refers to the environmental effects on our lives.	True False
3.	The babies' parents were from similar economic backgrounds.	True False
4.	The man who had a hard life thought it was mainly his own fault.	True False
5.	The nurse apologized for her mistake.	True False

DISCUSSION

According to a survey, about 10 to 12 percent of the adult population of Japan are estimated to be left-handed. With regard to handedness, what environmental factors affect this mostly genetic propensity?

A STEP FORWARD

Research online about the following genes and write a short summary.

novelty seeking gene
_____
_____

sirtuin gene
_____
_____

FURTHER READING

[1] アルバーツ、ブルース他（2016）。『Essential 細胞生物学』（原書第4版）中村桂子・松原謙一監訳、南江堂。
[2] 福岡伸一（2007）。『生物と無生物のあいだ』講談社。
[3] Watson, J. D. & F. H.C. Crick (1953). "Molecular Structure of Nucleic Acids: A Structure for Deoxyribose Nucleic Acid." *Nature* 171. pp. 737–738.
[4] ワトソン、ジェームス D. (2009)。『DNA のワトソン先生、大いに語る』吉田三知世訳、日経 BP 社。

[1] は多くの大学で分子生物学を受講する際の教科書として採用されている。専門用語についても丁寧に説明がなされており、分子生物学を学ぶ上では必携である。[2] は DNA の発見等、科学的大発見について興味深く書かれている本である。文章がリズミカルに書かれており、知的好奇心をかき立てる1冊である。[3] は DNA 二重らせん構造の発見を報告した原著論文である。X線構造解析にて二重らせん構造が美しく捉えられている。[4] は分子生物学者のワトソン博士が語った自叙伝的エッセイである。自身の生い立ちから研究者としての心構え等、ワトソン博士の意見がうかがえる1冊である。

LESSON 10
Women's Rights Are Human Rights

INTRODUCTION

　1975年メキシコシティで国際連合主催の国際婦人年世界会議が開催され、男女平等の促進、経済・社会・文化の発展への女性参加の確保、国際友好と世界平和に対する女性の貢献の重要性の認識という目的を達成するために、その後10年にわたる国内・国際両面における行動への指針を与える「世界行動計画」が採択されました。最終年にあたる1985年「国際婦人の10年」ナイロビ世界会議が開催され、西暦2000年に向けて各国等が効果的措置をとる上でのガイドラインとなる「婦人の地位向上のためのナイロビ将来戦略」が採択されました。第4回世界女性会議は、国際連合創設50周年にあたる1995年9月に北京で開催され、「北京宣言」および「行動綱領」が採択されました。この行動綱領によって各国政府は1996年末までに自国の行動計画を開発し終えることを求められました。以下、北京宣言の一部を抜粋します。

北京宣言（一部抜粋）
1　我々、第4回世界女性会議に参加した政府は、
2　国際連合創設50周年に当たる1995年9月、ここ北京に集い、
3　全人類のためにあらゆる場所のすべての女性の平等、開発及び平和の目標を推進することを決意し、
4　あらゆる場所のすべての女性の声を受けとめ、かつ女性たち及びその役割と環境の多様性に留意し、道を切り開いた女性を讃え、世界の若者の期待に啓発され、
5　女性の地位は過去十年間にいくつかの重要な点で進歩したが、その進歩は不均衡で、女性と男性の間の不平等は依然として存在し、主要な障害が残っており、すべての人々の安寧に深刻な結果をもたらしていることを認識し、
6　また、この状況は、国内及び国際双方の領域に起因し、世界の人々の大多数、特に女性と子どもの生活に影響を与えている貧困の増大によって悪化していることを認識し、
7　無条件で、これらの制約及び障害に取り組み、世界中の女性の地位の向上とエンパワーメント（力をつけること）を更に進めることに献身し、また、これには、現在及び次の世紀へ向かって我々が前進するため、決意、希望、協力及び連帯の精神による緊急の行動を必要とすることに合意する。

AIM & OBJECTIVE

CONTENT

　ヒラリー・クリントン氏が1995年に第4回世界女性会議で行った演説を読むことで、世界にはどのような女性問題が存在してきたかを理解し、さらにどのような行動をとるべきかについて考えていきます。

LANGUAGE

　このレッスンでは、メッセージを効果的に伝える方法、相手を説得して納得させる、また行動させる方法について学びます。また、リスニングではこのレッスンのトピックに関する講義を聞き、内容理解や要約などの訓練を行います。

READING: Women's Rights Are Human Rights

 ▶19

◆ Key Words & Phrases

human rights	人権。世界人権宣言 (Universal Declaration of Human Rights) は1948年12月10日の第3回国際連合総会で採択された、すべての人民とすべての国が達成すべき基本的人権についての宣言である。第1条で「すべての人間は、生まれながらにして自由であり、かつ、尊厳と権利とについて平等である。」と宣言されている。世界人権宣言は、この宣言の後国際連合で結ばれた人権条約の基礎となっており、世界の人権に関する規律の中でもっとも基本的な意義を有する。
women's suffrage	婦人参政権、婦人選挙権。アメリカ合衆国では、1848年ニューヨーク州セネカフォールズで開催された会議以降組織的に女性の権利を求める運動が始まった。婦人参政権運動家キャリー・チャップマン・キャット等の運動により1919年6月に婦人参政権を認める憲法修正第19条が可決。1920年8月28日に36の州で批准され発効。南部9州は憲法修正を否認した。
Declaration of Independence	（アメリカの）独立宣言（書）。北米の13の植民地がイギリスからの自由と独立を宣言したもので、1776年7月4日第2回大陸会議で採択。主にT.ジェファーソンが起草し、56人が署名。この日はアメリカの独立記念日 (Fourth of July) となる。しかし、当時の独立宣言書には、生命、自由、幸福の追求の権利を授けられるのは men, 政府も men の間に設けられるとされており、women は入っていなかったため女性の不満が募った。上述のセネカフォールズ会議において女性に対する不当な扱いのリストを作成した委員会は、アメリカの男性政府に対する女性の不満は、（独立前の）アメリカ人男性のイギリス国王ジョージ3世に対する不満と同じだけあると記している。

[1]　Our goals for this conference, to strengthen families and societies by empowering women to take greater control over their own destinies, cannot be fully achieved unless all governments—here and around the world—accept their responsibility to protect and promote internationally recognized human rights. The international

---

出典：Clinton, Hillary Rodham. September 5, 1995. "Remarks to the United Nations Fourth World Conference on Women." https://www.youtube.com/watch?v=xXM4E23Efvk　アメリカ合衆国のヒラリー・ロダム・クリントン氏が第4回世界女性会議で行った演説。会議に参加した世界各国の政府により北京宣言および行動要綱が採択された。

[1]　empower ... to do　「…に〜する権限を与える」

community has long acknowledged—and recently reaffirmed at Vienna—that both women and men are entitled to a range of protections and personal freedoms, from the right of personal security to the right to determine freely the number and spacing of the children they bear. No one should be forced to remain silent for fear of religious or political persecution, arrest, abuse or torture.

2 Tragically, women are most often the ones whose human rights are violated. Even now, in the late 20th century, the rape of women continues to be used as an instrument of armed conflict. Women and children make up a large majority of the world's refugees. And when women are excluded from the political process, they become even more vulnerable to abuse. I believe that now, on the eve of a new millennium, it is time to break the silence. It is time for us to say here in Beijing, and for the world to hear, that it is no longer acceptable to discuss women's rights as separate from human rights.

3 These abuses have continued because, for too long, the history of women has been a history of silence. Even today, there are those who are trying to silence our words. But the voices of this conference and of the women at Huairou must be heard loudly and clearly:

4 It is a violation of human rights when babies are denied food, or drowned, or suffocated, or their spines broken, simply because they are born girls.

5 It is a violation of human rights when women and girls are sold into the slavery of prostitution for human greed—and the kinds of reasons that are used to justify this practice should no longer be tolerated.

6 It is a violation of human rights when women are doused with gasoline, set on fire and burned to death because their marriage dowries are deemed too small.

7 It is a violation of human rights when individual women are raped in their own communities and when thousands of women are subjected to rape as a tactic or

---

[1] **recently reaffirmed at Vienna**　東西冷戦後の1993年ウィーンで開催された世界人権会議により採択された「ウィーン宣言および行動計画 (Vienna Declaration and Programme of Action)」のこと。世界のあらゆる人権蹂躙に対処するための、国際人権法や国際人道法に関する原則や国際連合の役割、すべての国々に対する要求を総括した宣言および行動計画である。この宣言および行動計画は同年国際連合総会において承認され、国連人権高等弁務官事務所が設置されることとなった。
[2] **entitle ... to ～**　「…に～の権利を与える」
[10] **refugee**　「(特に、宗教・政治上の迫害を避けるために国外へ脱走する) 亡命者、難民」
[11] **vulnerable**　「(精神的な) 害をこうむりやすい、(非難・攻撃などを) 受けやすい」
[17] **Huairou**　「懐柔区」北京市の市轄区。政府間会議と同時にNGOフォーラムが開催されていた。
[20] **spine**　「脊柱、脊椎、背骨」
[22] **prostitution**　「売春」
[24] **douse**　「浴びせる、びしょ濡れにする」
[25] **dowry**　「(新婦の) 持参金、持参の品物 (など)」

prize of war.

8. It is a violation of human rights when a leading cause of death worldwide among women ages 14 to 44 is the violence they are subjected to in their own homes by their own relatives.

9. It is a violation of human rights when young girls are brutalized by the painful and degrading practice of genital mutilation.

10. It is a violation of human rights when women are denied the right to plan their own families, and that includes being forced to have abortions or being sterilized against their will.

11. If there is one message that echoes forth from this conference, let it be that human rights are women's rights and women's rights are human rights once and for all. Let us not forget that among those rights are the right to speak freely—and the right to be heard.

12. Women must enjoy the rights to participate fully in the social and political lives of their countries if we want freedom and democracy to thrive and endure. It is indefensible that many women in non-governmental organizations who wished to participate in this conference have not been able to attend—or have been prohibited from fully taking part.

13. Let me be clear. Freedom means the right of people to assemble, organize, and debate openly. It means respecting the views of those who may disagree with the views of their governments. It means not taking citizens away from their loved ones and jailing them, mistreating them, or denying them their freedom or dignity because of the peaceful expression of their ideas and opinions.

14. In my country, we recently celebrated the 75th anniversary of women's suffrage. It took 150 years after the signing of our Declaration of Independence for women to win the right to vote. It took 72 years of organized struggle, before that happened, on the part of many courageous women and men. It was one of America's most divisive philosophical wars. But it was a bloodless war. Suffrage was achieved without a shot being fired.

15. But we have also been reminded, in V-J Day observances last weekend, of the

---

[3] **ages** 文法的には aged が普通だが、実際のスピーチのまま。
[6] **genital mutilation** 「性器切除」
[8] **abortion** 「妊娠中絶、人工流産、堕胎」
[8] **sterilize** 「不妊にする」
[11] **once and for all** 「これを最後に、きっぱりと」
[14] **enjoy** 「(人が)(特権など)を享受する」
[30] **V-J Day** 「(第二次大戦の連合軍の) 対日戦勝記念日 (*Victory over Japan Day* の略)」降伏調印日の1945年9月2日。イギリスでは日本が降伏を発表した8月15日をいう。

good that comes when men and women join together to combat the forces of tyranny and to build a better world. We have seen peace prevail in most places for a half century. We have avoided another world war. But we have not solved older, deeply-rooted problems that continue to diminish the potential of half the world's population.

16 Now it is time to act on behalf of women everywhere. If we take bold steps to better the lives of women, we will be taking bold steps to better the lives of children and families too. Families rely on mothers and wives for emotional support and care; families rely on women for labor in the home; and increasingly, everywhere, families rely on women for income needed to raise healthy children and care for other relatives.

17 As long as discrimination and inequities remain so commonplace everywhere in the world—as long as girls and women are valued less, fed less, fed last, overworked, underpaid, not schooled, subjected to violence in and outside their homes—the potential of the human family to create a peaceful, prosperous world will not be realized.

18 Let this conference be our—and the world's—call to action. Let us heed that call so we can create a world in which every woman is treated with respect and dignity, every boy and girl is loved and cared for equally, and every family has the hope of a strong and stable future. That is the work before you, that is the work before all of us, who have a vision of the world we want to see for our children and our grandchildren.

19 The time is now. We must move beyond rhetoric, we must move beyond recognition of problems, to working together, to have the common efforts to build that common ground we hope to see.

20 God's blessings on you, your work and all who will benefit from it. Godspeed and thank you very much. *(1064 words)*

---

[26] **godspeed** 「成功の祈願」人・企業の成功や旅行の無事などを祈る挨拶。

• Women's Rights Are Human Rights •

◆ Pre-class Task

Read the passage above. Mark each sentence as T (True) or F (False).

☞ 1

1. This conference can't be successful unless the internationally admitted human rights are supported and advanced by governments around the world. (　　)

☞ 2-3

2. Sadly, women's human rights have often been violated. (　　)
3. Women have long been abused because their history has not been spoken. (　　)

☞ 11-13

4. "Freedom" means respecting the opinions of people who might oppose the opinions of their government. (　　)

☞ 14-16

5. It was 72 years after the signing of the Declaration of Independence that women won the right to vote. (　　)

☞ 17-20

6. A peaceful and successful world will come true even if discrimination and unfairness are often found around the world. (　　)

◆ In-class Task

Warm-up

Work with your partner. Find the definition of these words in connection to speech:

　　rhetoric: _____
　　repetition: _____
　　contrast: _____
　　illustration: _____

Read the text above, and decide which type of rhetorical devices were used in Hillary Clinton's speech.

Discuss: Why did she use them?
　　　　　What was the effect on the listener?

• LESSON 10 •

How could she have said them differently?

Reading Comprehension

☞ ①

1. What did the international community reaffirm at the Vienna conference?

2. Find some concrete examples of human rights.

☞ ②

3. What should they declare in Beijing?

☞ ④–⑩

4. Give seven examples of human rights violations described in paragraphs 4 to 10 of the text (the first one is done for you).
   - ④ Babies are killed only because they are girls.
   - ⑤
   - ⑥
   - ⑦
   - ⑧
   - ⑨
   - ⑩

☞ ⑪

5. What is the message that comes from this conference?

☞ ⑮

6. What have we solved, and what haven't we solved?

110

• Women's Rights Are Human Rights •

☞ 16
7. What will happen if we take bold steps to better the lives of women?
_____
_____
_____

☞ 18
8. What is the vision of the world we want to see?
_____
_____
_____

☞ 19
9. What is meant by the words "we must move beyond rhetoric?"
_____
_____
_____

LISTENING: Equal Rights

▶ 20

Before You Listen

What words do you think of when you see these two pictures?

1.   2.

List the words here:
   1. _____   2. _____

111

• LESSON 10 •

Word Focus

What words or expressions do you think are important to understanding gender equality and equal rights? Write **6 words** connected to the topic and an **example sentence** using them.

equality (n.)	The goal of agreements like the Vienna Convention is equality for all people, regardless of their gender, race or ethnicity.

Listening 1: Short Summary

Listen to the passage and complete this summary of the listening using the following words in their correct forms (use 4 of the 5 words).

respect (v.)   law (n.)   opinion (n.)   change (v.)   opportunity (n.)

According to the speaker, the ability to _____ the world begins with encouraging more people to _____ the rights and _____ of others, and providing more _____ for all voices to be heard.

Listening 2: Question & Answer

Listen again to the passage and answer the following questions. You can use the box below to write notes.

1. What was the homework that the students should have completed before this lesson?

   _____

112

2. What is the first thing the speaker asks the students to think about?
   _____

3. What does the speaker recommend to help change our pre-conceptions about other people?
   _____

4. Why does the speaker ask the students to think about the people in their lives?
   _____

5. What does the speaker say people should do if other people say negative things?
   _____

Notes

True / False

Using your notes, discuss with your partner whether the following statements are true or false. Circle the correct answer and explain your decision.

1.	The speaker disagrees with Hillary Clinton.	True False
2.	The speaker reminds the students that society contains many different groups.	True False
3.	The speaker believes that everyone should think carefully about their own opinions.	True False
4.	The speaker says it is impossible to respect people you don't know.	True False
5.	The speaker recommends accepting everyone's opinions, even if they are negative or hurtful.	True False

DISCUSSION

Can you think of a situation in which men and women are treated unequally? List some situations and discuss in groups.

_____
_____
_____

A STEP FORWARD

Read and listen to the speech delivered by Malala Yousafzai at the Novel Prize Award Ceremony.

1. What is the message she wanted to convey to people all over the world?
2. How did she succeed in conveying her message effectively?

FURTHER READING

[1] クリントン、ヒラリー・ロダム (2007)。『リビング・ヒストリー——ヒラリー・ロダム・クリントン自伝』(上下巻) 酒井洋子訳、早川書房。

[2] ユスフザイ、マララ & クリスティーナ・ラム (2013)。『わたしはマララ——教育のために立ち上がり、タリバンに撃たれた少女』金子瑞人・西田佳子訳、学研マーケティング。

[3] 「マララ・ユスフザイ　ノーベル平和賞受賞記念講演」
http://www.nobelprize.org/nobel_prizes/peace/laureates/2014/yousafzai-lecture.html

[4] 「第4回世界女性会議　北京宣言」
http://www.un.org/womenwatch/daw/beijing/beijingdeclaration.html

[1] はヒラリー・ロダム・クリントンの自伝。イェール大学ロー・スクールを修了後弁護士として子供、女性、社会的弱者の権利擁護に力を注ぎ、ニクソン大統領弾劾の司法委員会にも参加。1975年ビル・クリントンと結婚。1993年大統領夫人になり、医療保険改革や女性の地位向上のために尽力した。このスピーチで語られた「沈黙の言葉は語られない」「女性の権利は人権だ」についても触れられている、力強い半世紀についての自伝であり、一読をお薦めしたい。[2] は「すべての子供に教育を」と訴え、2014年タリバンに銃撃されたが、一命を取り留め、2014年ノーベル平和賞を17歳で受賞したマララ・ユスフザイの手記。[3] はマララ・ユスフザイがノーベル平和賞受賞後に行った記念講演。分かりやすい英語でゆっくりと、しかし力強いメッセージを伝えており、これも全編を読んで聞くことをお薦めしたい。[4] 第4回世界女性会議で採択された北京宣言の全文が出ている。

LESSON 11 Black Holes and Astronomical Wonders

INTRODUCTION

　ブラックホールという言葉はほとんどの人が耳にしたことがあると思います。多くの人が抱いているブラックホールの素朴なイメージは、宇宙にあって、周りの物質を吸い込む、黒い天体…というものではないでしょうか。ブラックホールとはどのような天体で、宇宙のどこにあり、どのようなメカニズムで周りの物質に作用するの  かといったことは、20世紀初頭以降、物理学や天文学が発展する中で少しずつ理解が進んできました。特に近年では、高性能の宇宙望遠鏡がいくつも打ち上げられて観測の成果を蓄積することによって、これまでヴェールに包まれていたブラックホールの実像が次々に明らかになってきています。

　日本語や英語では、あまりにもスケールが大き過ぎて日常感覚では捉えられない状況を、「天文学的な（astronomical）」という言葉で形容します。ブラックホールについて知るには、文字通り天文学的なスケールの世界に思いを馳せなければなりません。それは、光、重力、時間など、私たちにとって当たり前の存在が当たり前でなくなる世界でもあります。ブラックホールを知ることは、私たちが生きている日常の意味を捉え直す機会にもなるでしょう。

AIM & OBJECTIVE

CONTENT

　このレッスンでは、ブラックホールがどのような物であり、他の天体にどのように作用するのか、また近年の研究成果によってブラックホールに対する理解がどのように変化してきたのか、といったことを学びます。

LANGUAGE

　宇宙で起きている物理現象は、我々が容易に想像できるようなものではありません。今回の文章は、科学的な説明や抽象的な記述を正確に理解するためのよいトレーニングになるでしょう。そのためにも、どの現象とどの現象が因果関係にあり、どの現象とどの現象が対比関係にあるかなどをきちんと整理して把握することが重要になります。また、リスニングで

はこのレッスンのトピックに関する講義を聞き、内容理解や要約などの訓練を行います。

READING: Amazing Black Holes

 ▶ 21

◆ Key Words & Phrases

supernova explosion	超新星爆発。質量の大きい恒星が起こす大規模な爆発で、それによってその星は一生を終える。
neutron star	中性子星。ブラックホールと同じく、超新星爆発を起こした恒星の核から作られる天体。
event horizon	事象の地平面。その中からは光すら出てくることができないという境界のこと。その中でどのような事象が起きているか知ることができないため、事象の地平面と呼ばれる。
gamma ray burst	ガンマ線バースト。電磁波の一種であり、きわめて高いエネルギーを有するガンマ線が、短時間のうちに放出され、鮮やかな閃光として観測される現象。

1. Don't let the name fool you: a black hole is anything but empty space. Rather, it is a great amount of matter packed into a very small area—think of a star ten times more massive than the Sun squeezed into a sphere approximately the diameter of New York City. The result is a gravitational field so strong that nothing, not even light, can escape. In recent years, NASA instruments have [5] painted a new picture of these strange objects that are, to many, the most fascinating objects in space.

2. Although the term was not coined until 1967 by Princeton physicist John Wheeler, the idea of an object in space so massive and dense that light could not escape it has been around for centuries. Most famously, black holes were [10] predicted by Einstein's theory of general relativity, which showed that when a massive star dies, it leaves behind a small, dense remnant core. If the core's mass is more than about three times the mass of the Sun, the equations showed, the force of gravity overwhelms all other forces and produces a black hole.

3. Scientists can't directly observe black holes with telescopes that detect x-rays, [15] light, or other forms of electromagnetic radiation. We can, however, infer the

---

出典：NASA. 2015. "Black Holes." http://science.nasa.gov/astrophysics/focus-areas/black-holes/ NASA（アメリカ航空宇宙局）のウェブサイトに掲載されている解説記事の一つ。インターネットを通じて幅広い読者に読まれており、宇宙に関する人々の知識と理解を深めるのに貢献している。

[12] **remnant**　「残骸」
[16] **electromagnetic radiation**　「電磁放射」このパラグラフ中で言及されているX線、光、ガンマ線などを総称して電磁波と呼ぶ。

presence of black holes and study them by detecting their effect on other matter nearby. If a black hole passes through a cloud of interstellar matter, for example, it will draw matter inward in a process known as accretion. A similar process can occur if a normal star passes close to a black hole. In this case, the black hole can tear the star apart as it pulls it toward itself. As the attracted matter accelerates and heats up, it emits x-rays that radiate into space. Recent discoveries offer some tantalizing evidence that black holes have a dramatic influence on the neighborhoods around them—emitting powerful gamma ray bursts, devouring nearby stars, and spurring the growth of new stars in some areas while stalling it in others.

4 Most black holes form from the remnants of a large star that dies in a supernova explosion. (Smaller stars become dense neutron stars, which are not massive enough to trap light.) If the total mass of the star is large enough (about three times the mass of the Sun), it can be proven theoretically that no force can keep the star from collapsing under the influence of gravity. However, as the star collapses, a strange thing occurs. As the surface of the star nears an imaginary surface called the "event horizon," time on the star slows relative to the time kept by observers far away. When the surface reaches the event horizon, time stands still, and the star can collapse no more—it is a frozen collapsing object.

5 Even bigger black holes can result from stellar collisions. Soon after its launch in December 2004, NASA's Swift telescope observed the powerful, fleeting flashes of light known as gamma ray bursts. Chandra and NASA's Hubble Space Telescope later collected data from the event's "afterglow," and together the observations led astronomers to conclude that the powerful explosions can result when a black hole and a neutron star collide, producing another black

---

[1] **matter** 「物質」
[2] **interstellar matter** 「星間物質」恒星間に存在する物質の総称。地上から星雲として観測されることもある。
[3] **accretion** 「降着」ガスなどが、質量の大きい天体の重力によってその表面に降り積もること。
[7] **tantalizing** 「興味をかき立てるような」
[8] **devour** 「吸い込む」
[9] **spur** 「…に拍車をかける」
[9] **stall** 「失速させる」
[20] **stellar** 「星の、恒星の」
[21] **Swift** 「スウィフト」NASA によって打ち上げられた宇宙望遠鏡で、地球の周りを回りながら天体の観測を行っている。
[21] **fleeting** 「ほんの一瞬の」
[22] **Chandra** 「チャンドラ」NASA によって打ち上げられた宇宙望遠鏡。
[22] **Hubble Space Telescope** 「ハッブル宇宙望遠鏡」NASA によって打ち上げられた宇宙望遠鏡。
[23] **afterglow** 「残光」

hole.

6   Although the basic formation process is understood, one perennial mystery in the science of black holes is that they appear to exist on two radically different size scales. On the one end, there are the countless black holes that are the remnants of massive stars. Peppered throughout the Universe, these "stellar mass" black holes are generally 10 to 24 times as massive as the Sun. Astronomers spot them when another star draws near enough for some of the matter surrounding it to be snared by the black hole's gravity, churning out x-rays in the process. Most stellar black holes, however, lead isolated lives and are impossible to detect. Judging from the number of stars large enough to produce such black holes, however, scientists estimate that there are as many as ten million to a billion such black holes in the Milky Way alone.

7   On the other end of the size spectrum are the giants known as "supermassive" black holes, which are millions, if not billions, of times as massive as the Sun. Astronomers believe that supermassive black holes lie at the center of virtually all large galaxies, even our own Milky Way. Astronomers can detect them by watching for their effects on nearby stars and gas.

8   Historically, astronomers have long believed that no mid-sized black holes exist. However, recent evidence from Chandra, XMM-Newton and Hubble strengthens the case that mid-size black holes do exist. One possible mechanism for the formation of supermassive black holes involves a chain reaction of collisions of stars in compact star clusters that results in the buildup of extremely massive stars, which then collapse to form intermediate-mass black holes. The star clusters then sink to the center of the galaxy, where the intermediate-mass black holes merge to form a supermassive black hole. *(828 words)*

---

[2]   **perennial**　「ずっと続く」
[5]   **stellar mass**　「恒星質量の（＝恒星程度の質量をもつ）」
[8]   **snare**　「捕まえる」
[8]   **churn out**　「大量に生み出す」
[12] **Milky Way**　「天の川銀河」太陽を含む恒星の集団のこと。「銀河系」とも呼ばれる。夜空に見える「天の川」は、天の川銀河を内側から観測することによって帯状に見えているものである。
[19] **XMM-Newton**　「XMM ニュートン」欧州宇宙機関（ESA）によって打ち上げられた宇宙望遠鏡。

• Black Holes and Astronomical Wonders •

◆ Pre-class Task

Read the passage above. Mark each sentence as T (True) or F (False).

☞ 1

1. A black hole is an empty space from which nothing can escape. (   )
2. Recently, NASA has succeeded in taking a picture of a black hole using their special instruments. (   )

☞ 2

3. Einstein's theory of general relativity had already predicted the idea of a black hole long before the term became famous. (   )

☞ 3

4. By using special telescopes, scientists can observe the effects black holes have on stars around them. (   )

☞ 4

5. When the surface of a large star nears the "event horizon," the star will start collapsing and disappear immediately. (   )

☞ 6

6. There are two radically different size scales of black holes: smaller ones are about 10 times as massive as the Sun, and larger ones are about 24 times as massive as the Sun. (   )

☞ 7

7. "Supermassive" black holes are as large as the Sun. (   )

☞ 8

8. Today, some astronomers believe that mid-sized black holes may form a supermassive black hole. (   )

119

• LESSON 11 •

◆ In-class Task

Warm-up

Following your reading of the text, try to draw an image of a black hole swallowing a star. Compare your drawing with your partner's.

Reading Comprehension

☞ 1

1. Fill in the blanks and complete the statement.

   A black hole is "black" because its force of gravitation is so _____ that _____

☞ 3

2. List at least four examples of black holes' effect on other matter nearby mentioned in this paragraph.

   _____
   _____
   _____
   _____
   _____

☞ 4

3. Select the correct answers to complete the description.

   After a supernova explosion, if the mass of the remnants of a star is A) { smaller / greater } than three times the mass of the Sun, it will become B) { a neutron star / a black hole }. On the other hand, if the mass is C) { smaller / greater } than three times the mass of the Sun, it will become D) { a neutron star / a black hole }, and E) { before / after } the surface of the collapsing star reaches an imaginary surface called the "event horizon," time on the star appears to stop for observers F) { deep inside / distant enough from } the surface.

☞ 5

4. What does "the observations" in this paragraph refer to?
   _____
   _____

☞ 6

5. Why are most stellar black holes impossible to detect?
   _____

☞ 7 - 8

6. Put the events in the correct order to describe a possible process of the formation of supermassive black holes.

   A) Formation of mid-sized black holes
   B) Development of extremely massive stars
   C) Merging of mid-sized black holes
   D) A chain reaction of collisions of stars in compact star clusters

   _____ ⇒ _____ ⇒ _____ ⇒ _____

• LESSON 11 •

LISTENING: Wonders of the Universe

 Before You Listen

What are some of the wonders that can be found in the Universe?

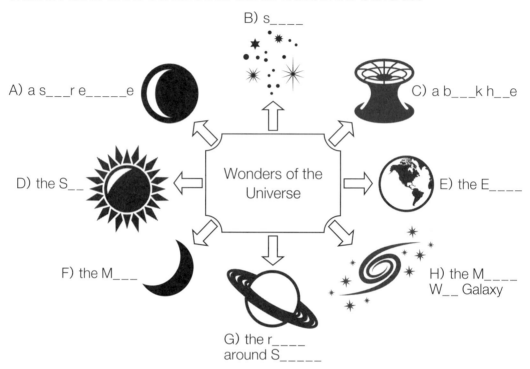

A) a s_ _ r e _ _ _ _ e
B) s _ _ _ _
C) a b _ _ _ k h _ _ e
D) the S _ _
E) the E _ _ _ _
F) the M _ _ _
G) the r _ _ _ _ around S _ _ _ _ _
H) the M _ _ _ _ W _ _ Galaxy

Word Focus

Choose **5 words** from the "Before You Listen" and write an **example** of how they are connected to your life.

Sun	Watching the Sun rise every morning makes me realize how lucky I am to be alive.

• Black Holes and Astronomical Wonders •

🎧 Listening 1: Short Summary

Listen to the passage and complete this summary of the listening using the following words in their correct forms (use 4 of the 5 words).

| wonder (n.) | solar (adj.) | Hubble Telescope (n.) | eclipse (n.) | Universe (n.) |

The vast _____, home to our planet Earth and the _____ system, is an amazing place full of _____ such as solar _____, black holes, and the Milky Way.

🎧 Listening 2: Question & Answer

Listen again to the passage and answer the following questions. You can use the box below to write notes.

1. What does "this vast spread of darkness" refer to?
   _____

2. According to the speaker, how is a star destroyed by a black hole?
   _____

3. How have technological advances changed the way we see the world?
   _____

4. Which image from outer space has become a cultural icon?
   _____

5. Why does the speaker mention the importance of the Earth's distance from the Sun?
   _____

Notes **Tip**: Numbers and dates are important when listening.

123

 **True / False**

Using your notes, discuss with your partner whether the following statements are true or false. Circle the correct answer and explain your decision.

1. It is dangerous to watch a solar eclipse with the naked eye.   True False
2. The speaker says that human life began with the Universe.   True False
3. The appearance of the Milky Way is caused by pollution in cities.   True False
4. The Hubble telescope was 25 years old in April, 2015.   True False
5. The speaker thinks that outer space is the most fascinating wonder of the Universe.   True False

DISCUSSION

What questions about the Universe do you think are yet to be answered? Write down your thoughts and share them with your partner.

    How old is the Universe?

    When will we find proof of other life in the Universe?

_____
_____
_____
_____

A STEP FORWARD

Find an online article reporting new findings or hypotheses about black holes and describe the findings in your own words.

_____
_____
_____
_____
_____

FURTHER READING

［1］ニュートン編集部（2010）。『ブラックホールと超新星—恒星の大爆発が謎の天体を生みだす』（Newton 別冊）ニュートンプレス。
［2］小山勝二・嶺重慎編（2007）。『ブラックホールと高エネルギー現象』（シリーズ現代の天文学 8）日本評論社。
［3］ホーキング、スティーヴン W.（1995）。『ホーキング、宇宙を語る—ビッグバンからブラックホールまで』林一訳、早川書房。
［4］佐藤勝彦（2008）。『宇宙論入門—誕生から未来へ』岩波書店。

［1］は、ブラックホールが超新星爆発により発生する原理を図解付きで分かりやすく説明している。また、ガンマ線バーストについての歴史がたどりやすい。他に、ブラックホールが他の天体に近づいた時に起こる現象や、ブラックホールの質量が2クラスに分かれる理由、時空のゆがみによる現象についても言及されている。［2］は、ブラックホールが及ぼす他の天体への影響について詳しい。降着円盤（ブラックホールに降着するガスで形成される円盤のこと）の生じる機構や、降着円盤がX線などを放射する理由について、力学的ポテンシャルやエネルギーの流れといった直感的な概念で説明している。［3］は「アインシュタインの再来」ともいわれる車椅子の天才科学者ホーキングが宇宙の神秘の解明について語った一般読者向けの解説書。この宇宙はどうやって生まれ、どんな構造をもっているのか。この人類の根源的な問いに正面から挑んでいる。［4］はインフレーション理論で有名な宇宙物理の第一人者による啓蒙的な著作。物理学の最先端と天文観測の最先端の100年間の紆余曲折が見通しよく語られている。

LESSON 12 What Is Literature?

INTRODUCTION

　私たちはふだん無意識のうちに「文学」とそうでないものを区別していますが、その区別はどのような基準にのっとっているのでしょうか。あるいは、そもそもそのような区別をすることは可能なのか、そうすることに何の意味があるのか。一見シンプルに思えるこれらの問いが、文学研究においてどう扱われているのか見てみましょう。

　「文学とは何か」は、文学研究における最も重要で最も難しい問題であると言えますが、このような答えにくい問いに、文学研究がどのように対処してきたのかを見ることで、より一般的に応用可能な論理的思考の方法を学ぶことができます。例えば、他との比較ではなく、「文学」そのものにはっきりした特徴があると仮定する方法があります。果たしてそのような「文学の本質」と言うべきものが存在するかどうかは、研究者の間でも意見が分かれるところですが、学術研究として文学を扱う以上、その研究対象の正体が分からないままにしておくのは、あまり科学的な姿勢であるとは言えません。

AIM & OBJECTIVE

CONTENT

　このレッスンでは、文学研究・批評と、その分野における最も大きな問いの一つ、すなわち「文学とは何か？」について読みます。それに加えて、なぜこの問いがそれほど重要なのかについても考えます。

LANGUAGE

　そのままでは扱いにくい大きな問いを、より小さく具体的な問いに分けて扱う方法を学びます。さらに、一見すると答えのなさそうな問題について考える際に、自分なりに工夫して問いを立てる（的確な疑問文を作成する）練習を行います。また、リスニングではこのレッスンのトピックに関する講義を聞き、内容理解や要約などの訓練を行います。

READING: What Is Literature and Does It Matter?

◆ Key Words & Phrases

literary theory	直訳すれば「文学理論」。広義には、作家が創作のために用いるアイデアや技法も含むが、文学研究においては、一般的には文学作品を解釈するための理論的枠組みのことを指す。文学だけに限定された理論もあるが、多くは他の思想や研究分野から導入された概念を含んでいる。
text	テクスト、テキスト。具体的には印刷された文字からなる文学作品の言語と内容を指すが、音楽や映画などを対象とする場合は、文字情報に限定されない。
discourse	言説（げんせつ）。何らかの物事について言われたり書かれたりしたものを総称する言葉。実際に何かを行う「実践 (practice)」と対比して用いられている。
narrative	物語、ナラティヴ。story と narrative はどちらも「物語」と訳されるが、文学研究ではこの2つは区別する。story は物語の内容（「何」が語られているか）で、物事の進行を指し、narrative は、物語の形式（「どのように」語られているか）に注目する概念である。

1. What is literature? You'd think this would be a central question for literary theory, but in fact it has not seemed to matter very much. Why should this be?

2. There appear to be two main reasons. First, since theory itself intermingles ideas from philosophy, linguistics, history, political theory, and psychoanalysis, why should theorists worry about whether the texts they're reading are literary or not? For students and teachers of literature today there is a whole range of critical projects, topics to read and write about—such as 'images of women in the early twentieth century'—where you can deal with both literary and non-literary works. You can study Virginia Woolf's novels or Freud's case histories or both, and the distinction doesn't seem methodologically crucial. It's not that all texts are somehow equal: some texts are taken to be richer, more powerful, more

---

出典：Culler, Jonathan. 1997. *Literary Theory: A Very Short Introduction*. Oxford: Oxford University Press. pp. 18–41.（邦訳：富山太佳夫・荒木映子訳『文学理論』岩波書店）作者のカラーはコーネル大学教授で、批評理論に関するすぐれた解説を数多く発表している。この記事は、入門書として書かれた本からの抜粋で、要点を押さえながらも簡潔で平易な文章で書かれている。

[4] **psychoanalysis**「精神分析（学）」
[7] **critical**「批評の」批評家は critic, 批評は criticism. 一般的用法と違い、必ずしも対象を批判するというニュアンスがあるわけではない。
[9] **Virginia Woolf** イギリスの作家・批評家（1882–1941）。
[9] **(Sigmund) Freud** オーストリアの精神医学者（1856–1939）。精神分析学の基礎を築いた。
[10] **methodologically**「方法論的に、やり方としては」具体的にどのような手順で、どのような道具を用いて分析するのか、ということ。

exemplary, more contestatory, more central, for one reason or another. But both literary and non-literary works can be studied together and in similar ways.

3   Second, the distinction has not seemed central because works of theory have discovered what is most simply called the 'literariness' of non-literary phenomena. Qualities often thought to be literary turn out to be crucial to non-literary discourses and practices as well. For instance, discussions of the nature of historical understanding have taken as a model what is involved in understanding a story. Characteristically, historians do not produce explanations that are like the predictive explanations of science: they cannot show that when X and Y occur, Z will necessarily happen. What they do, rather, is to show how one thing led to another, how the First World War came to break out, not why it had to happen. The model for historical explanation is thus the logic of stories: the way a story shows how something came to happen, connecting the initial situation, the development, and the outcome in a way that makes sense.

4   The model for historical intelligibility, in short, is literary narrative. We who hear and read stories are good at telling whether a plot makes sense, hangs together, or whether the story remains unfinished. If the same models of what makes sense and what counts as a story characterize both literary and historical narratives, then distinguishing between them need not seem an urgent theoretical matter. Similarly, theorists have come to insist on the importance in non-literary texts—whether Freud's accounts of his psychoanalytic cases or works of philosophical argument—of rhetorical devices such as metaphor, which have been thought crucial to literature but have often been considered purely ornamental in other sorts of discourses. In showing how rhetorical figures shape thought in other discourses as well, theorists demonstrate a powerful literariness at work in supposedly non-literary texts, thus complicating the distinction between the literary and the non-literary.

5   But the fact that I describe this situation by speaking of the discovery of the 'literariness' of non-literary phenomena indicates that the notion of literature

---

[1]　**exemplary**　「立派な、模範的な」
[1]　**contestatory**　「議論・論争を呼ぶような」
[1]　**central**　「中心的な」重要で不可欠であるということ。
[4]　**literariness**　「文学性、文学らしさ」literary（文学の）に -ness をつけて、抽象概念を表す。
[14]　**development**　「（ストーリーの）展開」始まりがあり、途中で様々な事が起こり（展開）、最後に結末があるというのが、伝統的な物語の形式。
[15]　**intelligibility**　「理解しやすさ」。
[22]　**rhetorical**　「修辞の、レトリックの」言葉を使って他の人々に働きかけ、特定の効果を生じさせるために用いられるテクニック（レトリック）に関する、という意味。
[23]　**ornamental**　「装飾的な、飾りに過ぎない」

continues to play a role and needs to be addressed.

6   We find ourselves back at the key question, 'What is literature?', which will not go away. But what sort of question is it? If a 5-year-old is asking, it's easy. 'Literature', you answer, 'is stories, poems, and plays.' But if the questioner is a literary theorist, it's harder to know how to take the query. It might be a question about the general nature of this object, literature, which both of you already know well. What sort of object or activity is it? What does it do? What purposes does it serve? Thus understood, 'What is literature?' asks not for a definition but for an analysis, even an argument about why one might concern oneself with literature at all.

7   But 'What is literature?' might also be a question about distinguishing characteristics of the works known as literature: what distinguishes them from non-literary works? What differentiates literature from other human activities or pastimes? Now people might ask this question because they were wondering how to decide which books are literature and which are not, but it is more likely that they already have an idea what counts as literature and want to know something else: are there any essential, distinguishing features that literary works share?

8   This is a difficult question. Theorists have wrestled with it, but without notable success. The reasons are not far to seek: works of literature come in all shapes and sizes and most of them seem to have more in common with works that aren't usually called literature than they do with some other works recognized as literature. Charlotte Brontë's *Jane Eyre*, for instance, more closely resembles an autobiography than it does a sonnet, and a poem by Robert Burns—'My love is like a red, red rose'—resembles a folk-song more than it does Shakespeare's *Hamlet*. Are there qualities shared by poems, plays, and novels that distinguish them from, say, songs, transcriptions of conversations, and autobiographies?
(820 words)

---

[13] **differentiate** 「区別する」
[23] **Charlotte Brontë**　イギリスの小説家 (1816–55)。妹の Anne と Emily も作家。
[24] **sonnet**　「十四行詩」詩の定型の一つで、様々なヴァリエーションがあるが、強弱のリズムが生じるように語を配置し、特定の場所で韻を踏むなどのルールに従う点で共通している。
[24] **Robert Burns**　スコットランドの国民詩人 (1759–96)。「蛍の光」の原曲 "Auld Lang Syne" を作詞。

● LESSON 12 ●

◆ Pre-class Task

Read the passage above. Mark each sentence as T (True) or F (False).

☞ ②

1. The author says that because we have so many things to do in modern society, we do not have much time to read literature. (   )
2. Works of literature and psychoanalysis can be studied in similar ways. (   )

☞ ③

3. Both literature and history can predict what happens in the future by logically examining what happened in the past. (   )

☞ ④-⑤

4. If there seems to be some features we call 'literariness', we should not ignore them when defining literature. (   )

☞ ⑥

5. 'What is literature?' and 'Does it matter?' are two clearly separate questions. (   )

☞ ⑦

6. More often than not, we already have an image of literature when we ask what literature is. (   )

☞ ⑧

7. The text of Shakespeare's *Hamlet* looks like a folk song. (   )

◆ In-class Task

Warm-up

The title of the article contains two questions: "What is literature?" and "Does it matter?" Scan the article to find 10 other questions and list them up (the first one is done for you). Compare your results with your partner's.

1. Why should this be?
2. _____
3. _____
4. _____

• What Is Literature? •

5. _____
6. _____
7. _____
8. _____
9. _____
10. _____

Reading Comprehension

☞ ①

1. What does "this" in the question "Why should this be?" refer to?
   It refers to _____
   _____

☞ ③–④

2. Why does the author mention other fields, such as history and psychoanalysis?
   He does this because _____
   _____
   _____

☞ ⑥

3. Does the author believe that we can define literature? Why or why not?
   {☐ Yes, he does / ☐ No, he doesn't} because _____
   _____
   _____

☞ ⑧

4. Why do you think the author ends this passage with a question?
   He does this because _____
   _____
   _____

131

• LESSON 12 •

LISTENING: Comparative Literature

 ▶ 24

Read these passages written by two famous 20th Century writers:

Passage 1

It was all very careless and confused. They were careless people, Tom and Daisy—they smashed up things and creatures and then retreated back into their money or their vast carelessness, or whatever it was that kept them together, and let other people clean up the mess they had made . . .

Passage 2

Where did you wash? the boy thought. The village water supply was two streets down the road. I must have water here for him, the boy thought, and soap and a good towel. Why am I so thoughtless? I must get him another shirt and a jacket for the winter and some sort of shoes and another blanket.

1. What do you think the central themes of both passages are? Why do you think so?
2. Look closely at the passages again. What do you notice about the style of writing?

Below are some important words and expressions that will help you to understand the listening. Write their **definition**.

comparative literature	
generate emotional content	
literary device/ literary style	
excerpt (n.)	
lavish (adj.)	
go slightly off topic	
winning (n.)	
classified advertisement	

Listening 1: Short Summary

Listen to the passage and complete this summary of the listening using the following words in their correct forms (use 4 of the 5 words).

> style (n.)   device (n.)   writer (n.)   literary (adj.)   reader (n.)

Understanding the writing _____ of an author can assist the _____ in analyzing a story, but more importantly, in understanding the _____ and his or her purpose for writing the _____ work.

Listening 2: Question & Answer

Listen again to the passage and answer the following questions. You can use the box below to write notes.

1. What is the purpose of the class?

2. Which two literary devices help the reader to visualize the story?

3. According to the speaker, why do writers use literary devices?

4. What are the two quoted passages about?

5. What other expression is used to describe the theory of omission?

Notes	**Tip**: A column format of note-taking is useful when comparing two situations.
Writer 1	Writer 2

• LESSON 12 •

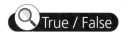 **True / False**

Using your notes, discuss with your partner whether the following statements are true or false. Circle the correct answer and explain your decision.

1. This is the final class of the course Comparative Literature 101.   True False
2. The writer's literary style is most remembered by readers.   True False
3. The speaker asked the students to listen to four separate passages.   True False
4. It was said that Hemingway's 6-word short story was written to win a bet in a bar.   True False
5. The Iceberg theory style of writing has been critiqued as lazy writing.   True False

DISCUSSION

Look at the list of questions you created in the "Warm-up" activity at the beginning of the reading section, and divide the questions into groups. Answer the questions below and share your results with your partner.

1. A) How many groups do you have? B) How did you divide the questions?
   A) _____ groups
   B) _____
   _____
   _____

2. What other questions will help you to think more critically about this issue? Write your own questions about the content of the text.
   _____
   _____
   _____

A STEP FORWARD

What is consciousness? To answer this big question, search online for several definitions of "consciousness" and divide the question into three smaller questions. (You may begin each with "What," "Why," and "How.")

Q1: _____

Q2: _____

Q3: _____

FURTHER READING

[1] Miller, J. Hillis (2002). *On Literature.* London: Routledge.
[2] 川口喬一・岡本靖正編 (1998)。『最新文学批評用語辞典』研究社。
[3] イーグルトン、テリー (2014)。『文学とは何か―現代批評理論への招待』(上下巻) 大橋洋一訳、岩波書店。
[4] ロッジ、デイヴィッド (1997)。『小説の技巧』柴田元幸・斎藤兆史訳、白水社。

[1] は文学研究というよりは、文学全般についての概説書。筆者はアメリカのイェール大学の研究者を主とする「イェール学派」の中心的人物で、アメリカにおける文学研究の重鎮的存在だが、本書には筆者の個人的な読書体験や、電子化が進む現代における読書についての考察などが盛り込まれており、比較的なじみやすい内容となっている。[2] は日本で編集された文学批評の用語解説辞典。文学研究に必要とされる概念や専門用語について、具体的な参考書を挙げながら的確で簡潔な解説がなされており、文学研究を志す者は、ぜひとも手元に置いておきたい1冊である。[3] は、イギリスの著名な文学者による、現代文学批評の歴史とその意義についての論考。文学をじっくり味わう素朴な読み方から、政治的テーマに踏み込んだ読解まで、過去100年間の西洋における文学研究の歩みを詳細に描き出している。筒井康隆の小説『文学部唯野教授』がこの本のパロディとなっていることも有名で、両者を読み比べてみても面白い。[4] は、イギリスの文芸批評家・作家による、小説がどのように書かれているのかを解説する本。文学作品をより深く楽しむために知っておくとよい様々な小説のテクニックが、トピックごとに、作品からの抜粋とあわせて紹介される。読書ガイドとしても役に立つ1冊である。

Acknowledgments

LESSON 1
From WHY THE BRAIN PREFERS PAPER. Reproduced with permission. Copyright © 2013 Scientific American, a division of Nature America, Inc. All rights reserved.

LESSON 2
From NAKED ECONOMICS: UNDRESSING THE DISMAL SCIENCE by Charles Wheelan. Copyright © 2010, 2002 by Charles Wheelan. Used by permission of W.W. Norton & Company, Inc. Audio and Japanese reprint arranged with Janklow & Nesbit Associates, New York through Japan Uni Agency, Inc., Tokyo.

LESSON 3
From EVOLUTIONARY PSYCHOLOGY: A BEGINNER'S GUIDE by Robin Dunbar, Louise Barrett & John Lycett. Copyright © 2005 by Robin Dunbar, Louise Barrett & John Lycett. Used by permission of Oneworld Publications.

LESSON 4
From SOFT POWER by Joseph S. Nye, Jr. Copyright © 2004 by Joseph S. Nye, Jr. English reprint arranged with Perseus Books Group, USA through Tuttle-Mori Agency, Inc., Tokyo. Japanese reprint arranged with Curtis Brown Group Ltd, London through Tuttle-Mori Agency, Inc., Tokyo. Japanese and English Audio reprint arranged with ICM/Sagalyn, Washington D.C. through Tuttle-Mori Agency, Inc., Tokyo.

LESSON 5
From HUMAN FACTORS IN TRAFFIC SAFETY by Robert E. Dewar, Paul L. Olson. Copyright © 2007 by Robert E. Dewar, Paul L. Olson. Used by Permission of Lawyers & Judges Publishing Company, Inc., c/o Copyright Clearance Center.

LESSON 6
From METAPHORS WE LIVE BY by George Lakoff & Mark Johnson. Copyright © 1980 by The University of Chicago Press. Used by Permission of The University of Chicago Press.

LESSON 7
Cartoons by Seppo Leinonen. Used by permission of Seppo Leinonen.

LESSON 8
From ROSA PARKS: MY STORY by Rosa Parks with Jim Haskins. Copyright © 1992 by Rosa Parks. Used by permission of Dial Books for Young Readers, an imprint of Penguin Young Readers Group, a division of Penguin Random House LLC. Audio reprint arranged with The Betsy Nolan Literary Agency.

LESSON 9
From LIVING WITH OUR GENES by Dean Hamer & Peter Copeland. Copyright © 1998 by Dean Hamer & Peter Copeland. Used by Permission of Doubleday, an imprint of the Knopf Doubleday Publishing Group, a division of Penguin Random House LLC. All rights reserved. Audio reproduction by permission of Dean Hamer, Ph.D. through Tuttle-Mori Agency, Inc., Tokyo.

LESSON 12
From LITERARY THEORY: A VERY SHORT INTRODUCTION by Jonathan Culler. Copyright © 1997 by Jonathan Culler. Used by permission of Oxford University Press.

Photos
p. 1: © Dmitry Lobanov; p. 9: © logo3in1; p. 13: © miw45kg; p. 21: © adam121; p. 25: © NoraDoa; p. 32: © Neyro; p. 36: © Andrea Izzotti; p. 47: © VRD; p. 56: © RioPatuca Images, © nao5970; p. 60: © Rzoog; p. 92: © rosendo; p. 122: © Stoyan Haytov, © kuroksta, © antto, © Sam, © jongjawi; p. 126: © tony4urban
Cover: © leszekglasner, © moonrise, © Andrew Kazmierski, © Monet, © beeboys, © sivivolk, © spiritofamerica, © Sergey Nivens, © ArTo, © dejah_thoris

AUTHENTIC READER
A Gateway to Academic English
オーセンティック・リーダー

● 2016 年 8 月 1 日　初版発行 ●
● 2021 年 3 月 17 日　4 刷発行 ●

● 著者 ●
Academic English Textbook Editorial Committee
Faculty of Languages and Cultures
KYUSHU UNIVERSITY
九州大学大学院言語文化研究院 学術英語テキスト編集委員会
Copyright © 2016 by Kyushu University

● 発行者 ●
吉田尚志

● 発行所 ●
株式会社 研究社
〒 102-8152　東京都千代田区富士見 2-11-3
電話　営業 03-3288-7777（代）　編集 03-3288-7711（代）
振替　00150-9-26710
http://www.kenkyusha.co.jp/

KENKYUSHA
〈検印省略〉

● 装丁デザイン ●
ナカグログラフ（黒瀬章夫）

● 本文デザイン ●
株式会社インフォルム

● 印刷所 ●
研究社印刷株式会社

● 音声録音・編集 ●
（株）東京録音

ISBN978-4-327-42196-0 C1082　Printed in Japan

本書の無断複写（コピー）は著作権法上での例外を除き、禁じられています。
また、私的使用以外のいかなる電子的複製行為も一切認められておりません。
落丁本・乱丁本はお取り替えいたします。
ただし、古書店で購入したものについてはお取り替えできません。